PATRIOTISM AND PROHIBITION

———oOo———

ADDRESSES AND ARTICLES

by

B. H. CARROLL, D.D., LL.D.,

Pastor, First Baptist Church,
Waco, Texas,
and
First President of the Southwestern
Baptist Theological Seminary,
Fort Worth, Texas

———oOo———

COMPILED AND EDITED

by

J. W. CROWDER, A.B., E.B., D.D.

43,973

FOREWORD

These addresses and articles on Patriotism and Prohibition were delivered by the author during the mighty conflicts with the evil forces of the Liquor Traffic over a space of several decades and offer to the present generation something worthwhile on the subject as applicable to the issues of to-day.

It will be noted that these discussions have been compiled and arranged on the basis of the relation of the two themes to each other. According to the author Patriotism and Prohibition are inseparable, therefore the reader will find a blending of the two ideas in these discussions.

The reader should read Dr. Carroll's two sermons — one on "The Whisky Traffic" and the other on "Prohibition" — in his volume of "Sermons on Christian Education and Some Social Problems," pp. 116 to 173.

There are some gems of literature here. It is doubtful as to whether the author's addresses on "Our Country's Flag," "The First Amendment and Its History," "The Liquor Traffic" (His Reply to R. Q. Mills), "Governor Ross Answered," "Personal Liberty," and "The Prohibition of the Liquor Traffic," have ever been surpassed.

We joyfully express here our appreciation of the co-operation of our good friend, E. Holbrook Waterman, who has made possible this volume of addresses and articles by his voluntary contribution.

Surely these addresses and articles have application to modern political and social conditions to-day.

March 15, 1952.

> J. W. Crowder,
> Seminary Hill,
> Fort Worth, Texas

TO

ALL LOVERS OF RIGHTEOUSNESS

THIS VOLUME IS RESPECTFULLY

DEDICATED BY THE

EDITOR

CONTENTS

CONTENTS (Con.)

I

THE HEROINES OF 'THIRTY-SIX

(A speech written by Dr. Carroll for a school girl.)

How can a school-girl write an original historic essay that will be interesting or profitable? I shall not try it. If permitted, I prefer to read a selection hitherto unpublished.

It was the fault of ancient history that it recounted only the achievements of the great or rich or titled. It glorified the knights, barons, kings and plutocrats. The masses of the people who suffered most, toiled most and were protected least—these were referred to only in a few, general terms and then simply as a background in a picture setting off by contrast the glory of a single person. Very gradually and to only a limited degree as yet has the fault of this method been abandoned by the historians.

This fact is manifest in the extant histories of Texas and in all our annual celebrations of great events. We imitate the past. We gather flowers and make laurels to crown the brows and to perpetuate the memory of a very few, until by an excess of adulation we surfeit the people with monotonous repetitions and echoes. The result is that we nauseate the public stomach by too frequent overdoses of the same over-sweet adulation of the same few names and thereby defeat the very purpose of our partial praise. A reaction sets in. Great names become a jest and a spirit of irreverence succeeds to over-much discriminating laudation.

If we would truly foster a general spirit of patriotism, if we desire even to keep green the memory of the very few names we seek to make illustrious and if we would make our celebrations truly entertaining and profitable, and if we would be just, these desirable results can be attained only by diversifying our annual celebrations. No two or three dozen names make a nation. "There were great men before Agamemnon" and have been since. Would it detract from the real fame of the few names generally lauded, would it not give freshness and variety to our now tame and spiritless celebrations, *that are sometimes so monotonous,* if occasionally we devoted an anniversary exclusively to hitherto unmentioned names of the rank or to phases of our Texas revolution so long shaded into background? Are not the unfrequented nooks or retired valleys sometimes sweeter to visit than crowded shrines or dusty thoroughfares? Was not that the peculiar charm of the writings of Washington Irving and Robert Burns and Dickens; and I say it very reverently, was it not the crowning glory of the method of that Jesus of Nazareth who both modestly served and exalted the people? The nurturing power of a natural spirit of the sweet home life and rural scenes depicted by Irving, the Cotter's Saturday Night by Burns, the pathos by Dickens, who left to "Lothair" the toadying to "My Lords and Parliament" while he illumined the tenement houses of the suffering poor, and the matchless example of our Lord who turned away from "Rabbi, Pharisee and Scribe" to compassionate the "sheep without a shepherd" — these all admonish us to change our methods.

Let these displace those. In the necessarily short space alloted to one essay I can but indicate and not elaborate. I have gathered my flowers for San Jacinto celebration. They are not hot-house roses and geraniums. They are but wild violets and verbenas, hawblooms, wild-pinks and buffalo clover — a modest garland — but I would place it on the unmarked grave of some wife or daughter or sister unmentioned in history — whose virtues illumined the log-cabin of long ago, who yoked the oxen — who barred her door by night against wild-beast and wilder savage and in lovely unrecorded courage stood sentinel with her rifle over the baby in the crude cradle — while husband or brother or father was far away on the perilous scout.

You, my unknown sisters, are the heroines of 'thirty-six. If the spirits in yonder world can see us here, you will recognize my wild prairie flowers and woodland wreath. They are such as you knew in life. You knew nothing of modern luxuries and improvements. You never saw a Brussels carpet or a hat from Paris. What you wore, your own toil-roughened fingers fashioned out of the fabrics of loom or the skins of wild-beasts. What you ate you cooked yourself, having raised your bread and slain your game. You were not afraid of night or solitude or Mexican or tramp or Comanche. You were an ignorant soul — never dreaming that you were a heroine and wholly unconscious that you were laying the foundations of a great nation.

Your husband perished, perhaps on some solitary scout or in some unarmed skirmish with Mexican or Comanche. History omits his name. Like Moses, no man knows where he is buried. You were left without neighbors, in a wilderness, a widow without time to grieve, because you were a mother whose little children heard the wolf howling by night or might be waked by warhoops or Mexican "Carramba." Hail Sister — All hail — heroine of 'thirty-six! See the flowers I bring to hallow your memory. You will recall them. They are not modern exotics — strangers to your life. Barefooted or shod in Moccasins you walked among them many a glorious spring-morning long before barbed wire ever girdled and fettered your free prairies. You never saw a lane and cared nothing for roads. The sun was your clock — the north star your compass and the constellations your almanac.

Again I say: Daughter of Freedom and Mother of Liberty — all hail! Again I say, look at my woodland wreath: wild peach, hawthorne blossoms, blades of grass and wild-plum blooms that suggest the hum of the wild bee, the song of the mocking-bird or the scream of the plover.

O Texas Sister, on this anniversary I turn from the monotonous echoes of past laudations which glorify *ad nauseam* just a few names, no more deserving of praise than yours, and seek in the wild wood, or lonely motte of timber, or mountain side or rolling prairie for some unmarked grave, noted only by the all-seeing eye, and there if I could identify it, I would place my modest wreath of Texas flowers and grasses, and thus decorate the mold enriched by unchronicled, but sublimely heroic dust.

II

OUR COUNTRY'S FLAG

(An address delivered at a Flag-Raising at Baylor University, October 24, 1896.)

Thirty-six years ago, this very month, and pending the stormy presidential election in November, 1860, whose issue precipitated disunion and civil war, the patriotic boys of Baylor University upreared on the public square of Independence, Texas, just such a cloud-piercing flagstaff as these Baylor cadets have erected here, from its summit unfurled the "Star-Spangled Banner." From that hour until this moment, when youth and beauty pull the tackle that sends the same fluttering bunting to yonder peak, that flag has not floated as the University ensign.

It was uplifted then in the face of a gathering storm which soon shut out heaven with blackness and deluged the land with fratricidal blood. It was greeted then with mingled cheers and hisses.

It was my fortune then, a schoolboy of seventeen, to deliver the oration on the occasion of that last unfurling of "Old Glory" by a civilian's hand on Texas soil, prior to the outbreaking of the colossal "War between the States." It was my fortune then to recite, with all a schoolboy's fervid rhetoric, Cutter's poetical paraphrase of the words of Henry Clay, speaking from the pedestal of Bunker Hill monument. Fragments of that poem, after the lapse of thirty-six years, I thus recall:

> "You ask me when I'd rend the scroll
>   our fathers' names are written o'er—
> When I could see our flag unroll its
>   mingled stripes and stars no more;
> When with a worse than felon hand, or
>   felon counsel, I would sever
> The union of this glorious land — I
>   answer: Never! Never!

— 11 —

"Think you that I could brook to see
    that banner I have loved so long,
Borne piecemeal o'er the distant sea,
    or trampled by a frenzied throng—
Divided — measured — parceled out —
    tamely surrendered up forever
To gratify a soulless rout? I answer:
    Never! Never!

"Dissolve the Union! God of Heaven! We
    know too well how much it cost.
A million bosoms shall be riven — ere
    one golden link be lost.
Upon yon column's marble base — that
    shaft which soars into the sky,
There still is room enough to trace the
    countless millions yet to die.

"And I would cover all its height, breadth,
    before that shame,
'Till space should fail whereon to write,
    e'en the initials of a name.
There let it stand until the river that
    flows beneath shall cease to flow;
Aye, until that hill itself shall quiver,
    with nature's last convulsive throe."

So spoke the schoolboy of 1860 while his heart was aflame with the conflicting feelings excited by "Bleeding Kansas," John Brown's Raid, Uncle Tom's Cabin, Helper's Impending Crisis, the rending of the Democratic Convention at Charleston, and the heroic failure by the Baltimore convention in the nomination of John Bell of Tennessee and Edward Everett of Massachusetts.

Following that banner scene at Independence, where the intrepid Baylor boys were girdled by a hostile populace, there came, in quick and startling succession, the plurality election of Abraham Lincoln, the secession of the Southern states, the organization of the Southern Confederacy, and such a civil war, in the cost of blood and treasure, as the world has never known. The South heroically fought it out to the last ditch and the last man against overwhelming odds, "robbing the cradle and the grave" for the "materiel and personnel" of its last army corps. Following the fortunes of my own state, I enlisted in the first Confederate regiment and surrendered with the last. And surrendering accepted loyally, once and for all, the bloody verdict of war's arbitrament.

By a strange coincidence it is my fortune now, pending another stormy presidential election, to see my son, a Baylor University cadet, and other Baylor students, sons of the boys who in the long ago backed me so bravely under that other flag, gathered here to raise and unfurl once more — and I trust forever — the same "Star-Spangled Banner" as the ensign of Baylor University. And by a yet stranger coincidence, it is my fortune now, as then, to deliver the oration at the unfurling of the flag. And with the same spirit that animated my young heart in 1860, I now point to that same flag and cite the burning words of Oliver Wendell Holmes:

> "Behold! Its streaming rays unite,
> One mingled flood of braided light:
> The red that fires the Southern rose,
> With spotless white from Northern snows;
> And, spangled o'er its azure, see
> The sister stars of Liberty;
> Then hail the Banner of the Free,
> The starry Flower of Liberty."

Now, happily, only cheers do greet it. And I venture to say cheers as hearty and loyal from these war-scarred relics of the "Boys in Gray" as come from the lips of these other war-scarred remnants of the "Boys in Blue." Following up the foregoing exordium I may be allowed, I trust, to impress on these youthful minds some pertinent facts of history.

Let not the young people suppose that yonder flag fluttered over Prescott's head or dying Warren on Bunker Hill. The Banner displayed at Washington's headquarters before Boston had indeed the thirteen stripes, meaning colonies only, while its square field of blue was marked by symbols of British rule. Old Ethan Allen carried not this flag when he demanded the surrender of Ticonderoga in the name of God and the Continental Congress. Montgomery and Arnold bore it not in the assault on Quebec.

Washington's standard-bearer showed not these colors on Long Island, on the doubtful field of White Plains, nor when crossing the Delaware on the floating ice he struck the Hessians at Trenton and the subordinates of Cornwallis at Princeton. It was not this flag which Sergeant Jasper replaced in the thick of battle on the thunder-riven walls of Fort Moultrie and afterwards planted on Savannah's parapets and yet afterward wrapped around him as a bloody shroud.

You must bear in mind that the National Declaration of Independence was not signed till July 4, 1776, and it was more that a year afterward before the young nation had adopted and proclaimed a flag. Try to fix the following dates and fact in your minds: On June 14, 1777, Congress decreed: "That the Flag of the thirteen United States be thirteen stripes, alternate red and white; that the union be thirteen stars, white in a blue field, representing a new constellation." But this decree was not officially promulgated until September 3, of that year.

So we may suppose that Washington's first battles under this flag were on the disastrous fields of Brandywine and Germantown, the one preceding, the other succeeding the British occupation of Philadelphia.

The first recorded instance of the presence of

this flag, which I am now able to recall, was just after the decisive battles of the Revolution, when Sir John Burgoyne surrendered to Gates at Saratoga. History does say of that event, that when the long line of British and German troops defiled through the opened columns of their stalwart conquerors that they there witnessed the unfurled folds of the star-spangled banner which Congress had just decreed as the National ensign.

But in 1794, after the reception into the Union of Vermont and Kentucky, there came, by decree of Congress, this change in the flag: "From and after May 1, 1795, the flag shall be fifteen stripes and fifteen stars."

It was this new flag that Hull ignominiously surrendered at Detroit over Lakes Erie and Champlain, that floated at the masthead of "Old Ironsides" in her naval victories, that Jackson behind his cotton bales triumphantly defended at New Orleans against Wellington's Peninsular veterans.

A still later change came, April 4, 1818, when Congress, by a final decree, to become operative July 4, 1819, reverted to the original thirteen stripes, with the addition of a new star for every state entering the union, each new star taking its place in the constellation on the first 4th of July after the admission of the state which it represented.

Now, boys, such being an outline of the history of the flag, let me fix in your minds, with the reasons therefor, some of its several names:

First, from its triple colors, you see them there, it is called "The Red, White and Blue." Second, from its azure, star-lighted field, it is called "The Star-Spangled Banner." Third, from its heroic memories it is called "Old Glory."

And now that you know something of its history and its name, permit me to propound and answer five questions on its symbolism:

First. It is the symbol of what? Look at it for yourselves. There are thirteen stripes united and forty-five stars united. Does that mean thirteen men united or forty-five people united? No. Not any number of men united. But it symbolizes states united. It says nothing of the comparative size or relative population of these several states. Indeed, we know that no two of them are equal in area or population. Look at your maps and compare little Rhode Island with mammoth Texas, or thick-peopled New York with the sparsely settled Nevada. Don't forget that. The flag tells of States United and hence the nation's name is not Columbia, nor America, but the United States of America.

Second. Now look at the flag and tell me from its speaking face, how many States were first united. How may you tell from the flag? Answer: Count the stripes. Thirteen stripes — thirteen States.

Let every child learn to tell off on his or her fingers, before night, the names of the original thirteen States, and to point them out on the map.

Third. Look again at the flag and tell me how many states now? How can you tell? Count the Stars. Forty-five stars — forty-five States.

Fourth. Again look at the flag and tell me the relation of the States toward each other, or rather the lesson of their combination. Mark you, the stripes are all painted on one piece of bunting. Mark you, the stars are grouped in one field of blue. What means it? You have only to recall the words of the original decree of Congress: "That the Union be thirteen stars, white in a blue field, representing a new constellation."

Fifth. Looking at the flag one more time, let us hear this question: If both stripes and stars represent states, what is signified by their difference in number — the one thirteen, the other forty-five? That means growth, the development, the increase of the nation.

Not one of the original thirteen stars has been blotted out, but from time to time in the last hundred years, other stars of the first magnitude, as brilliant as the first, have burst out of the gloom of night and taken their places in the glorious galaxy. States carved out of the territory freely given to the union by some of the first thirteen, or out of the later territory acquired by purchase and treaty.

So the flag, by its comparative thirteen and forty-five, either tells or suggests all the story of the purchase by Jefferson of the immense Louisiana territory, of the gain by the annexation of mighty Texas, with its sale of surplus territory enough for a nation, of the acquisition by treaty from Mexico, and Wm. H. Seward's purchase from Russia of that great Alaska, fertilized by the mighty Yukon, where "the lone wolf howls on Alaska's shore."

What a voice, then, has that flag! Over what strange seas and landscapes have its stars been shining and its stripes waving! What glorious victories by land and sea! It has been planted nearest the North pole. There in polar ice it was "unfurled and froze" while mingling the sheen of its stars with the radiance of the Aurora Borealis. The Algerine and Tripolitan pirate saw it and trembled. The Comanche and Sioux have heard its victorious flutterings over their wigwams in the boundless prairies and interpreted the sound as the rush of the wings of the avenging angel. Japan and China have greeted it. England, proud mistress of the seas, has witnessed from her own shores, her own standard lowered to it in equal frigate action.

We come now, young cadets of Baylor University, to consider the most important question of all — one upon which you cannot afford to be ignorant or misinformed.

The office of the flag — I would not have you regard that standard as "a mere painted rag." Nor cherish it as the symbol of "a mere poetic sentiment." More — much more than these does it signify. Let us particularize somewhat:

1. It is a symbol of nationality. The ship that

carries no flag on the high seas is justly treated as a pirate. No flag is the same as a black flag. The man without a flag is an Ishmaelite: "His hand against every man and every man's hand against him."

2. It is a symbol of national authority. It waves over all federal forces and forts and property. It is over the halls of national legislation, over every custom house and post-office. The mob that defies a sheriff or the municipal police trembles at one flutter of that flag. However insignificant in itself, so long as it stands for national authority you may not call it "a bauble." You recall the scene depicted in history, when Cromwell, escorted by mailed warriors, entered the house of parliament and pointing to the speaker's mace, contempuously said, "Remove that bauble!" and how a patriot leaped to his feet and cried: "You may count the days till England's freedom dies when you remove that bauble."

3. It is a declaration of principles. The proverb, "Show your colors," means: Declare your principles; align yourself. One glance at a flag on the high seas discovers the nature of the government it represents. You know at once whether that flag represents an autocracy, a monarchy, an oligarchy or a republic. By the flag you may determine the institutions of a nation and the very principles by which its government is administered.

4. It is a rallying point in times of confusion and danger. Oftentimes on desperate fields where chaos reigned and ruin was imminent, when the thunder of murderous guns and the mingled shoutings of adverse combatants drowned the voice of command, it has sufficed to plant the standard where danger menaced, where a final stand must be made, and its silent folds streaming out in the dim clouds and lurid flashes of war have uttered to the eye this saving voice: "Rally round the Flag!"

With what aptness and pathos does Macaulay

illustrate the power of this thought in his poetical paraphrase of the heroic words of Henry IV of France at the battle of Ivry:

> "And should my standard-bearer fall —
>   as fall full well he may,
> For never saw I promise yet of such
>   a bloody fray —
> Press where you may see my white plume
>   shine amidst the ranks of war,
> And be your Oriflame to-day — the
>   helmet of Navarre."

5. It is a symbol of protection to the helpless citizen in foreign lands. Long and pathetic would be the story of the instances where that flag, floating over an unarmed consulate in foreign lands, has been a barrier, not only to mob-violence but to the regular battalions of tyranny, more potent than granite fortifications crested with heavy artillery. As the ancient city of refuge sheltered the fleeing man-slayer from the avenger of blood, so that alone has been sufficient to guard the humblest and poorest citizen of the United States from violence wherever he may roam in the inhabited world.

6. It is a symbol of home to the wanderer. Our people are travelers. They go everywhere. For recreation or in the interest of science or trade they penetrate all jungles, climb all mountains, explore all seas. But as time passes, distance lengthens and barriers intervene, the heart grows sick with loneliness and longing. How sweet to such a wanderer when coming in sight of the sea to catch, as the gleam of the seagull's wing, the uplifting of a coming sail, or mark the first faint puff of cloud emitted from a steamer's throat and then from the mast-head behold the streaming folds of the star-spangled banner! As by the touch of a magician's wand, the sight of that flag recalls his own, native land. Rises up before the weary exile his own vine-covered cot-

tage with all the dear, familiar, domestic scenes far, far away. His heart melts, his tears overflow and he blesses the flag of his country for the memories of home it revives in his lonely heart.

Such, young gentlemen, are some of the offices of the flag which your patriotism has erected over this campus, and in view of these offices allow me next to answer three other questions:

First. Why unfurl this flag in the South? If for no other reasons, certainly these: To show that all bitter memories excited by the great civil war, from first Manassas to Appomattox, are buried in the deep sea of Oblivion. That the results of that war's bloody arbitrament are loyally accepted. That the "Boys in Gray" now meet the "Boys in Blue," not in "battle's magnificently stern array," but in mutual admiration of the devotion to sacred principle evinced by each, and to weep together over the fallen heroes of either side, as together they decorate the graves of their dead. That, pending another stormy presidential election, the whole world may know that we here will respect and uphold the verdict of the ballot, whatever that may be, and are for the Union, the whole union, one and indivisible.

Second. Why unfurl this flag over a school? Because one of the highest offices of a school is to teach patriotism to the young, and no other one thing in the world is more suggestive of patriotism than the nation's flag. From that flag they learn to love the whole country. Not merely from personal attachment to the place of one's birth, not from love of the mere natural features of our country, whether "fields, forests, streams, or mountains," but from devotion to its institutions and the great principles of liberty and happiness undergirding them. Such teaching of the lessons imparted by the flag bear fruit unto self-sacrifice, courage, liberality and unselfish devotion to the public welfare. So instructed, our young people become acquainted with the inspiring history of our country, familiar with its institutions, and are led to take an active and intelligent interest in public affairs and to hold as inestimable the sacred franchise of honorable citizenship.

Third. Why unfurl this flag over a Christian school? Because from the Christ himself, his people have learned to honor and obey the powers that be, as ordained of God, to pay tribute, to pray for all that are in authority, that we may lead a quiet and peaceable life in all godliness and honesty.

Finally, young men, as I commenced with an exordium so I close with a peroration. When God created the heavenly bodies he said: "Let there be lights in the firmanent of the heaven to divide the day from the night; and let them be for signs and for seasons and for days and years." Hence in all literature, sacred and profane, they are treated as "signs."

All our astronomies and almanacs appoint certain constellations as signs of the Zodiac, marking the successive seasons of the changing year. There are many of these constellations, arbitrary groupings of stars, such as Orion, Ursa Major, Taurus and the Pleiades, or Seven Stars, a smaller constellation in the neck of Taurus. These all, by figure of speech at least, are supposed to exert in turn their respective influence, favorable or sinister, on this earth. So in Job, that oldest book, Jehovah himself says: "Canst thou bind the sweet influence of the Pleiades, or loose the bands of Orion? Canst thou bring forth Mazzaroth in his season? Or canst thou guide Arcturus with his sons?"

And so the conception underlying yonder group of stars, represents a constellation, which burst upon a darkened world Anno Domini 1777 in response to another divine voice: "Let there be lights in the firmament of heaven and let them be for a sign."

In accord with that conception may I not apostrophize yonder flag, in the words of a gifted woman:

> "Stream, Old Glory, bear your stars
> High among the Seven;
> Stream a watchfire on the dark
> And make a sign in heaven."

A sign of "liberty, equality and fraternity." A sign before which tyrants tremble and crowns crumble. A sign that there shall no longer be an adulterous union of church and state. A sign that every man shall enjoy unmolested his inalienable right to worship God according to the dictates of his own conscience. A sign that the young Occident is carrying on the wings of example and suasion to the effete or moribund monarchies of the Orient the undying principles of a government "of the people, for the people, by the people."

Therefore, well may I now speak and well may you endorse the sentiment:

> "The Star-Spangled Banner! Forever may
> it wave
> O'er the land of the Free and the home
> of the Brave."

III

SOME REMINISCENCES OF THE WAR BETWEEN THE STATES WITH ITS ANTECEDENTS

(An address, place unknown, Dec. 11, 1906.)

I am asked to give my reminiscences of the war between the states — the most colossal human struggle, not only in modern times, but in all times.

Thucydides was able to immortalize himself by his classic story of the puny Peloponesian War — a war between petty Greek states — because his history was bigger that the war. But there can be no Thucydides of our war between the states. Myriads of historians, novelists, bards, sculptors, and painters only efface themselves in attempting to describe this titanic tragedy, as a black night in dismal swamps swallows up the hovering fireflies whose momentary flashes vanish in deeper darkness. Milton's war between the angels in Paradise Lost, followed not by his feebler Paradise Regained, but followed by Dante's Inferno, might somewhat approximate the magnitude and horrors of certain stages of this subject — preliminary stages only — because following this war has been not only no Paradise Regained to either North or South, but the subsequent Inferno of Destruction in the South, so mockingly called "Reconstruction," is very far from being the last volume of the tragedy.

Unfortunately the story is an endless serial, the coming effect of whose ultimate sequel our children's children must face, if they are able, but whose record so far is only vague, ominous, and minatory prophecy, a storm-cloud gathering thick, thunder-throbbing, lightning-gored, pushing up above the rim of the whole circle of the horizon — how much of it yet invisible below that rim God only knows and in mercy hides from our sight.

And I am asked to give my reminiscences of

such a war, a war rooting in past ages and fruiting in future ages. One insignificant unit out of millions, speaking from the view point of one experience out of millions, what can he do to enlighten on such a subject? Well, be it so — but remember that this generation is only in the middle volume of the serial, if indeed it be so far along. Remember it was this war with its antecendents and aftermaths that gave rise to colossal private fortunes in the North that by contrast make Croesus a pauper. It gave rise to trusts before which not only individual competition but even states are but as fine dust in the balances. It gave rise to the spirit of commercial gambling and greed that know no patriotism, no respect for human rights and no fear of God. It gave rise to an unrighteous pension roll, larger now after a lapse of more than forty years from the firing of the last gun than the armies of the war and ever increasing with no politician brave enough to speak the truth about it. It gave rise to the present race problem, many fold more complicated, more insoluble and more menacing than slavery prior to 1861. It gave rise to the destruction of vital elements of the old Constitution. Through its colossal fortunes heaped upon the few and its consequent wealth distinctions between classes, it gave rise to the present irrepressible conflict between organized capital and organized labor and to the day of strikes in every department of industry.

Remember that these and ten thousand other evil results of that war survive now and evince no symptoms of descreptitude. The law of consequences is as inexorbable as the law of gravitation. But you say the war has ceased. Yes, powder burning ceased at Appomattox, but we are yet paying for that burnt powder with other burnings and so far have not been able to meet the annual interest on the debt.

QUALIFICATIONS FOR REMINISCENCES

It is impossible to discard altogether the personal element from reminiscences but references to that element will be small. My previous political alignments and studies qualify me to indulge in reminiscence now. By education, at least, I was an old line Whig. My political text-books were the Federalist, the Madison Papers, the Speeches of Henry Clay and Daniel Webster. The Old South of my boyhood I know better than the New South now. You, of the present day, can never realize that South as I knew it.

In June, 1856, when something over twelve years old, I recited as my examination declamation that part of Webster's reply to Hayne published in the McGuffey readers. I literally gushed with sentiment in my delivery. I made my voice ring as I reiterated his eulogium on Massachusetts: "Her past, at least, is secure." And my imagination soared as I described his suppositious gathering of the birds of prey "to pick at, hawk at and tear" the grand old commonwealth, and fairly scraped dust from the stars as I solemnly rehearsed his climax — "The Union — one and indivisible."

When I went triumphantly to my seat I was considerably let down by an old man's saying: "Sonny, I reckon you don't know that four or five years ago Massachusetts went back on Daniel Webster and broke his heart, because he denounced her actual nullification laws, as disruptive of the union."

On the 27th of December 1858, when just fifteen years old to a day, I arrived in Texas to find the atmosphere charged with the conflict between Hardin R. Runnels and Sam Houston. In June 1859, I delivered a speech on Sam Houston which brought on me the censure of the Democratic board of trustees of the school at Caldwell. In 1860 at Baylor University I helped raise the last star-spangled banner that floated over Texas before the war, and

standing upon a goods-box in the street and facing
an excited opposition crowd that threatened to be
a mob, I delivered my last school boy speech in favor
of the Union. In April 1861 I entered the Confederate service, serving four years by the time I was
old enough to vote.

Throughout the war I studied its phases of development and made many speeches on its issues.
After the war I passed through all the phases of
reconstruction. And though since entering the ministry I have had nothing to do with politics, yet as
a citizen I have profoundly studied the aftermaths
of the war and have been compelled to reverse some
of my earlier judgments.

> "The mills of God grind slowly,
> But they grind exceedingly small."

When the last dust of this grinding has fallen into
the bin, it will be evident whose was the responsibility for this dreadful war. This evidence will appear in the distribution of punishment — even, exact,
final and irreversable justice, meted out by the
"Judge of all the earth who will do right," having
no respect for persons or sections. Did you say His
verdict is already rendered? Be not so easily de-
ceived. Was the verdict all in when Jerusalem was
destroyed by Babylon? In part only for Jerusalem;
none yet for Babylon. Jerusalem was restored and
for a thousand years heard the owl hoot, the bittern
scream and the jackal howl in the waste places
where once Babylon stood. Jerusalem lived to see
lions whelp in the crumbling palaces of Babylon.

That you may be prepared somewhat for the
ultimate verdict, historic consideration must be
given to certain terms written on my memory in
letters of fire — terms which when defined and applied contain the elements of the final verdict. These
terms are: The Constitution; Tariff for Protection;
Bounties; Subsidies; Slavery; Slave Trade; Aboli-

tionist; War to Free Slaves; Rebellion; Nullification; Secession. In dealing with these pregnant terms no Southern statesman or historian will be quoted. They have an equal right to be heard but will not be heard in this discussion. Indeed, in the excess of caution, no quotation from Northern historians either will be cited that has not passed through the ordeal of delivery before the Grand Army of the Republic and accepted as fact.

SLAVERY

Let us commence with the term "Slavery." Slavery in American history is divided into three parts:

First, slavery imposed upon conquered or stolen Indians. This slavery was confined mainly to the North. You know what "Wall Street" means now, but it derives its name from a wall erected for the purpose of preventing outraged Indian tribes from rescuing Indian slaves held by the white men. The Commissioners of the Colonies brought a grievance once against the Dutch in New Netherlands, now New York, and that grievance was that the Dutch harbored a fugitive Indian woman who had escaped from New England slavery. Many thrilling romances have been written by Northern men showing the horrors of this slavery.

The second slavery was the slavery of white people. This was slavery imposed mainly upon the Colonies of the Atlantic sea board by England. These white slaves constituted a mixed class, some were paupers, some were political prisoners and some were kidnapped. The romances of Mary Johnson entitled, "To Have and To Hold" and "Prisoners of Hope" deal with this White Slavery. But England was not alone to blame for this White Slavery. Reverse the ominous date 1861 and we have the date 1681. In 1681, in a secret session of the Massachusetts General Court, inspired by the clergy, a plot was matured to waylay and capture William Penn, "the scamp," as they called him, and one hundred "heretics, malignants and Quakers" in order to sell them into slavery for rum. Dr. Cotton Mather, the most important man in Boston and who was up to his eyes in this plot, thus justifies it: "Much spoil may be made by selling the whole lot to Barbadoes where slaves fetch good prices in rum and sugar and we shall not only do the Lord great service by punishing the wicked but shall make great gain for his ministers and people." He innocently signs himself, "Yours in the Bonds of Christ, Cotton Mather." (See documents in Massachusetts Historical Society.)

Third, the slavery of African people. Here dates are significant. In 1636, the first American-built slaver, the Desire, was sent out from Marble Head, Massachusetts and for *nearly two hundred years thereafter* New England increased her merchant marine, brought about her naval supremacy and added vastly to her wealth by importing and selling slaves. Newport, the present fashionable resort, laid the foundations of its great fortunes in the slave trade. One respectable Elder of Newport was in the habit of giving thanks in the meeting on the next Sabbath after a slaver arrived "because a gracious, overruling Providence had been pleased to bring to this land of freedom another cargo of benighted heathen to enjoy the blessings of the gospel dispensation." Samuel Hopkins of Rhode Island, in his Reminiscences says that in 1770 Rhode Island alone had one hundred and fifty ships in the African slave trade. The newspaper advertisements of negro sales in Boston in that time surpass anything ever seen in Southern newspapers. Negro children were sold "by the pound as other merchandise" or "given away like puppies." This iniquitous slave trade carried on for nearly two hundred years by New Englanders accounts largely for the wealth and naval supremacy of that section.

In colonial days Virginia twenty-three times voted to abolish the slave trade and each time their enactment was vetoed by the King on the petition of Massachusetts slave dealers. In 1733 Georgia prohibited the importation of slaves. In 1761 South Carolina according to Bancroft prohibited slavery. In 1775 a clause in the orginal draft of Jefferson's Declaration of Independence put among the grievances of the Colonies the veto of the King on this prohibitory Slave legislation, which was stricken out at the instance of a Massachusetts member. In 1782-3 Southern members in the Constitutional Convention urged the insertion of a clause abolishing the slave trade, but at the instance of Massachusetts members the slave trade was extended twenty years, until 1803, in fact until 1808.

Here is the crucial fact which establishes responsibility for African Slavery in America. In 1828 there were in America 140 Abolition societies, of which 103 were in the South and none in Massachusetts. The first abolition paper was published in Tennessee in 1828. In 1831 William Lloyd Garrison found the sentiment against abolition stronger in Massachusetts than in the South and more intolerant. In 1833 in a Connecticut town a woman opened a school for colored girls. The legislature prohibited it and the woman and her school were mobbed and other indignities perpetrated that to-day seem incredible. In 1835 William Lloyd Garrison attempted to organize an abolition society of thirty ladies in Boston. They were mobbed and the mob wore broadcloth. In 1835 George Thompson, another abolitionist, was mobbed in Augusta, Maine, and others in Concord, New Hampshire, in Lowell and Lynn, Massachusetts. Just three years after this, 1838, a bill to abolish slavery in the Virginia General Assembly failed to pass by just one vote.

When, then, we consider the sentiment in the South in the days of the establishment of slavery and in the days of the two hundred years of the iniquitous slave trade and the attitude during that period of the slave dealers of New England, we are prepared to get at the heart of the responsibility for African slavery in the United States. In later days when Henry Clay was asked by a Northern Abolitionist why he did not free his own slaves, he replied, "I will give them manumission papers whenever you are prepared to give them good legal security that you will take care of them." It is customary now in some quarters to regard the war which commenced in 1861 as a war to free slaves. There is not a word of truth in it. It is disproved by Mr. Lincoln's Inaugural Address March 4, 1861, in which he solemnly declares that he has no purpose, no right and no inclination to interfere with slavery in the states. To the same effect is a Congressional Resolution signed by the President in July, 1861. The manumission proclamation of Abraham Lincoln was an after-thought and a war measure only. You might call manumission a result but certainly not the cause of the war. The verdict of history is unequivocal that the South was little responsible for African slavery and that most heroically they had tried to roll back the tide of slave dealing. They made the best that they could of an unpleasant situation. We pass on to the term,

REBELLION,

and enumerate in order the rebellions in the history of the United States. First, the Revolutionary War was a rebellion unquestionably up to the Declaration of Independence in 1776. During the war there was a rebellion of the soldiers of the Pennsylvania Division commanded by Gen. Antony Wayne. In 1786, what is known as Shay's rebellion took place in Massachusetts. It was put down by President Washington through Gen. Lincoln. In 1794 there was a whisky rebellion in Pennsylvania. This was put down by the president through Gen. "Light Horse" Harry Lee, the father of Robert E. Lee. He commanded 15,000 men in suppressing this rebellion.

In 1812 occurred the great rebellion of New England. The war of 1812 in Madison's administration was undertaken to right the wrongs perpetrated upon New England seamen. But in the prosecution of that war there did develop an insurrection that amounted to the proportions of a Rebellion in New England. Governors refused to send troops to fight the British, even when the capital at Washington was threatened and was actually captured and burned. Legislatures passed resolutions obnoxious to the prosecution of the war. Troops were organized to be used against either the United States or Great Britain as the case might be, and unquestionably help was extended to the British by prominent Federalists in New England. Information was communicated and received by blue lights along the coast. Massachusetts by legislature resolution declared her right to resume her position as an independent state. A convention was held at Hartford, looking to severing the relations between New England and the United States. This rebellion ceased because peace came and not because it was ever put down. In 1857 there was a Mormon rebellion. This was put down by Gen. Albert Sidney Johnson, a Texan in command of the United States Army. In 1859 the rebellion at Harper's Ferry was put down by Gen. Robert E. Lee. These are the rebellions of United States history unless we add the insurrection in Chicago put down by Grover Cleveland. We now take up the term,

SECESSION.

Beyond all question secession originated in New England and the election of Thomas Jefferson was regarded and stated as sufficient ground for secession. Such is the declaration of Gov. Walcott of Connecticut. The Louisiana Purchase by Jefferson was made the occasion of kindling secession fires all over New England. John Quincy Adams is the authority that there was a plot and a plan to bring about this secession, that it was openly stimulated by the press and a Convention of New England states at New Haven was proposed. It is customary now in all the North to laud Alexander Hamilton. But when in 1804 he was dying from the bullet of Aaron Burr, he sent a message to Boston urging them if they would not break his heart to stop trying to disrupt the Union. Fiske in his Critical Period calls attention to the fact that the New England states demanded as a price for remaining in the Union that the mouth of the Mississippi should be closed to navigation for twenty-five years. Indeed the perpetuity of the union at the time of the Louisiana Purchase was perhaps saved by giving up the Texas part of the Louisiana Purchase.

In 1805 the Governor of New Hampshire published a document giving the names of prominent New England men whose purpose was to dissolve the union. In 1811 when the bill came up before Congress to admit Louisiana as a state only the utmost tact and delicate treatment accompanied by large concessions prevented the secession of the New England states. Julius Hawthorne, a Massachusetts author of celebrity, quotes the words of Josiah Quincy, in the United States Congress, more treasonable than any that ever fell from the lips of Southern sons and representatives in the days of '61. As has already been stated, the secession of the New England states was prevented only by the peace that followed the war of 1812. In 1845 when the Bill was up for the annexation of Texas, Ex-president John Quincy Adams and many others openly announced that the reception of Texas justified the dissolution of the ties which bound New England to the United States. In 1844-45 Massachusetts legislature affirmed that it was not bound to recognize the action of Congress. In 1850 Daniel Webster declared that it was the purpose of many in New England to dissolve the union.

We combine now the word,

NULLIFICATION,

with secession and unquestionably there is a connection between them. Nullification was the cause of the Southern secession in 1861. But it was not the nullification talked about in the great debate between Webster and Hayne. It was not the South Carolina nullification for that existed only as a threat. It was actual nullification in the personal liberty bills adopted by many Northern states. In 1851 Mr. Webser lost the prestige of his great debate with Hayne, in Massachusetts and in all New England, because he opposed nullification by the Northern states which set aside the principles of the constitution, the decisions of the Supreme Court and the action of the general Congress. Mr. Webster openly declared in this last great canvass that he made and the fruitlessness of which broke his heart, "If the North refuses to put aside these nullification enactments, I solemnly declare that the South has sufficient cause and just right to secede." The crisis came when a book entitled, Helper's Impending Crisis, openly inciting servile insurrecton was endorsed by sixty-three Northern members of Congress, including William H. Seward. But the climax became acute when John Brown invaded Virginia and took possession of the United States arsenal at Harper's Ferry, imprisoned men and committed murder. The climax exploded when for this act John Brown was canonized as a saint. He remains in the canon of the saints until this day.

The citations here given are attested each, by one or the other, of the following Northern histories: Bancroft's History of the United States, Bryant's History of the United States, Julian Hawthorne's History of the United States, Fiske's Critical Period, Documents of the Massachusetts Historical Society, Moore's History of Slavery in Massachusetts and others. Hundreds could have been cited but the limitation was confined to these because every one of them appears in an address before an encampment of the Grand Army of the Republic at Evansville, Ind., and was delivered by a Baptist preacher well-known to me and once a prominent pastor in Texas.

When the constitution was thus regarded as "a covenant with death and a league with hell," when congressional action was nullified by many Northern states, when the decision of the Supreme Court was disregarded and despised, when Southern soil had been invaded, when the invader and murderer was canonized as a saint, and when a president was elected by a partisan section and by a party which gloried in the facts cited, then the southern states seceded, but did not rebel. There was first a deliberate state resumption of state powers and a declaration of severance under all the forms of law and the constitution of a New Republic, by virtue of the inherent right of revolution, and every hopeful measure adopted to prevent war. Nothing was done, not absolutely essential to self-preservation.

It is not the present purpose to discuss the other terms named, to wit: Subsidies, Bounties and Protective tariffs, but merely to state that in the judgment of southern statesmen all these enriched one section at the expense of the other. I could not fairly give reminiscencies if I left out the general southern sentiment on these points:

1. That African Slavery would never have attained large proportions in the south but for the nearly two hundred years of slave trade forced upon its people.

2. That, as piracy on the Spanish Main built up the British navy, so the New England slave trade gave that section its foundation of wealth and the superior power of a merchant marine.

3. That Subsidies, B o u n t i e s and Protective tariffs largely increased this sectional wealth and added immeasurably to its mechanical and manu-

facturing powers and put it far ahead in transportation by land and sea.

4. That war-contracts and subsidies to great railways increased this wealth to such stupendous proportions that it passed beyond governmental control.

5. The demoralization resulting from plundering southern cotton, sugar and tobacco during the war would not cease with the war, and such wholesale destruction of private property as characterized the vandalism in the Shenandoah Valley and in the March to the Sea would brutalize a generaion at least.

6. That the stealings and plunderings of the reconstruction period were shocking to the moral sense of the world and would at some time bring awful retribution.

7. That the disregard of the terms under which Lee and Johnson surrendered and the disregard of the solemn promises of Abraham Lincoln that if manumission of slaves was accepted, followed by a return to the union, no other terms would be required — vitiated men's confidence in the good faith of the Nation. But some of these are aftermaths.

One reminiscence is more vivid than the events of yesterday. It was in 1862. About 15,000 Texans were pouring into Arkansas, following thousands who had preceded them. Our column had approached my boyhood home, Monticello, Drew County, Arkansas. About four years had elapsed since I left it. The citizens called upon me for a war-speech in the court-house. My heart thrilled as I looked out over an audience whose every face was familiar. They were wild with enthusiasm and feeding on what I considered illusory hopes. The war to them was a holiday excursion. I thought it necessary to dispel these illusions. I could to-day almost repeat that speech verbatim. I spoke nearly two hours with the solemnity deepening with every additional point made in the discussion. I loved these people and they loved me. Every word was in earnest and many of them in tears.

My theme was an adapted phrase of Patrick Henry's great address before the Burgesses of Virginia: *It is better to know the worst and to provide for it. No good comes from indulging in delusive phantoms of hope.* I close with a synopsis of that speech:

1. My first point was giving the distance from Austin, Texas, to Monticello and the remaining distance to Little Rock and thence to White River where the enemy were.

Over this distance our 15,000 infantry must march afoot. How much time such a march required and what an awful cost for wagon transportation and supplies. That the south had very few railways running east and west and no water-transportation. That it must defend a frontier reaching from the Rio Grande to the Atlantic Ocean.

It was therefore impossible to concentrate rapidly on any exposed point of that interminable frontier. That there was no natural boundary of defence which a few might hold until more came. That the North had many railways running east and west and limitless water-transportation. That we had an exposed water-front of many thousands of miles and that the secret military success lay in rapid concentration of overpowering forces at the point of attack.

2. That the trend of our navigable rivers was generally from north to south. That the Mississippi was our great weakness. Through superior naval power the confederacy might be cut in two. Then all west of the Mississippi would be left as a negligible quantity. From this section came the great supplies of beef, horses and mules.

3. That from the Mississippi their gunboats could ascend every navigable tributary into the heart of the Confederacy.

4. That we had no factories.

5. That already, through the blockade, supplies of necessary war-munitions were failing.

6. We had no arms except what we captured from the enemy.

7. That to try to hold forts or towns would entail many awful surrenders.

8. That there was no hope in Northern Democrats — what they attempted only increased the power of the radicals. In revolutions, radicals came to the front as scum rises to the top of boiling pots.

9. That there was no hope in European intervention.

10. That there was no hope in cotton without a market, and no way to keep the value of our currency unless we could get the cotton to European markets.

11. That with all the territory abandoned we lost recruiting ground and sources of supply.

12. That our supply of men was limited and a long war would call out the last reserve.

13. That we must depend upon ourselves alone and our hope lay in rapid and aggressive war.

As to the accuracy of the statements herein made, I leave all judgement on that to the students of history and as to the effects of this speech I leave that to the imagination of all who hear me to-day.

IV

THE FIRST AMENDMENT AND ITS HISTORY

(An address delivered at the B. Y. P. U. Convention, Baltimore, Md., July 20, 1895.)

I count myself happy in being permitted to speak this day to so vast a concourse of American youth on a great historic subject. History teaches lessons and imposes corresponding obligations. It is that lamp of experience which lights our way into the dark and pathless future. Very valuable is this light to young people, who until they acquire sufficient personal experience, must shape their course of life by authority, tradition and education. Fortunately the records of history can be made very attractive to the youthful mind.

No chain of facts in the history of the human race surpasses in interest and instruction tnat series of events which led to the formation of the constitution of the United States, a constitution which has been declared by competent and disinterested authority to be "The most wonderful work ever struck off at a given time by the brain and purpose of man." And no other event in the series equals in importance the adoption of that part of the first amendment, "Congress shall make no law respecting an establishment of religion, or prohibiting the free exercise thereof." Indeed this was the most revolutionary proposition of statecraft ever incorporated by man into organic law. It not only contradicted both the theory and practice of all existing governments, but was absolutely without precedent in the cycles of history, and all the shadowy realm of unwritten tradition.

Individual peaks are usually but somewhat higher elevations of the connecting mountain range, but this amendment, the loftiest eminence on the historic shores of time, without connection with a neighboring spur, or even mole-hill of the past, and with little graded approach to its own base, lifts itself up abruptly from the plain a sheer perpendicular of amazing height, and there stands isolated, unique, sublime. It is easy enough to find historical precedents for every other item of the first ten amendments, commonly called the Bill of Rights, but this had no model in the past.

Divesting ourselves of the light of the past century, and from the standpoint of contemporaries contemplating this amendment as a hitherto untried experiment, a logical mind is irresistibly driven to one of two conclusions: either the doctrine of this amendment is fallacious, because as a governmental measure it is opposed to universal human experience, or its author is God, and its communication a revelation.

Destroy my distinctive Baptist faith, and the pressure of history will constrain me, even now, to say that it is a failure as a governmental measure, propped up indeed for awhile by extraordinary circumstances and adventitious aids, yet doomed to fall when these props decay. But retaining my distinctive Baptist faith, I regard it as a concrete expression of that abstract spiritual truth enunciated nearly two thousand years ago by Jesus of Nazareth: "God is a Spirit, and they that worship him must worship him in Spirit and in truth." "My kingdom is not of this world." "Render unto Caesar the things that are Caesar's and unto God the things that are God's." To Baptists, therefore, this fraction of the first amendment must ever remain the brightest star in the galaxy of the Bill of Rights.

The history of its incorporation in the Constitution and of the part thereof performed by our Baptist fathers is of transcedent interest, and well worthy of this great occasion. But my theme, as scheduled on this program calls for impossibilities. The naked skeleton of the story cannot be articulated in the time given, much less is there opportunity to clothe the dry bones with flesh, and breathe into the body the breath of life. The roots of any history are deep under ground, and wide spreading its branches above. But this history is exceptionally complex in root, stem and branch. A knowledge of the history of all Europe for two hundred years preceding is essential to an intelligent conception even of the multiform problem. Omitting for the present all remoter facts, we may, however, construct in a few sentences this naked outline.

About the middle of the eighteenth century Great Britain controlled the Atlantic slope of the North American continent from the North Pole to Florida, and right heavy rested her hand of authority on her possessions. Thirteen of her American colonies associated themselves for the purpose of mutual counsel and defence against the oppressive government of the mother country. The first organ of general colonial defence was the old Continental Congress, which was organized September, 1774. This body, as the war progressed, issued a Declaration of Independence, July 4, 1776, the colonies thereby assuming to become free and independent states.

On the 15th of November, 1777, this congress of deputies formulated articles of confederation, which vested in a congress the general direction of affairs. But as the theory of their revolution was in opposition to a strong central government, they naturally restricted to very narrow limits the powers conferred on this congress. Indeed, so feeble were these powers that while it is always comparatively easy to invoke and temporarily associate destructive forces, yet the colonies were hardly able in eight years with the aid of France, to pull down and overturn, until they were actually, as well as declaratively, free from foreign control.

The provisional treaty of peace acknowledging their independence was signed by English plenipotentiaries and became operative January 20, 1783. But when, with peace, the hour of construction arrived, experience had already demonstrated that the powers of Congress were inadequate to such a purpose, and that the bonds of federation were weaker than the ropes of sand. While necessity, ever an imperious dictator, pointed with pitiless finger to an unpaid army waiting, with musket and sabre in hand, for some settlement before disbandment; pointed to foreign creditors clamorous for their long-deferred pay; to an empty treasury, without efficient means of providing a revenue; to loss of confidence at home and abroad; to an enormous issue of unredeemed paper money, bottomed on nothing, and depreciation to zero; to the impoverishment and demoralization of eight years of ruthless war, rapine and internecine strife. So pointing, the same necessity, with inexorable logic, shut up all thoughful men to one alternative — speedy remedy or anarchy.

The problem condensed itself into a nutshell: how can be constructed a central government strong enough for efficiency and with dignity enough to inspire respect without creating a possible tyrant in the central government, liable to take the state and the individual by the throat? By tardy processes, which time fails me to recite, the discussion of the situation eventuated in a Constitutional Convention, which met in Philadelphia, May 17, 1787, and closed its labors on the 17th of September of the same year. The compromise product of this convention was our present Constitution, minus all of its amendments.

This famous document was now referred to the moribund Congress, to be by it transmitted to the several state legislatures, that they in turn might submit it, for ratification, to conventions of the people of their respective states. These several state conventions, called forth for this express purpose, by their respective legislatures, each for itself and in its own time and way, did eventually ratify the Constitution, thereby superseding the old articles of Confederation. The new government under this Constitution went into effect March 4, 1789, over twelve states. Rhode Island had not as yet ratified the Constitution nor had participated in its formation. The first ten amendments, commonly called the Bill of Rights, were all adopted by the new government in the first term of Washington's administration, though not ratified afterwards by three of the states. The first amendment dates in congressional action September, 1789.

This outline as a preface, leads up to the general feature of my theme, the history of the first amendment. Suppose before you, our Constitution with all of its present amendments. You will observe that an amendment seems to be a simple matter of a few words and easily written. But it required one and a half million men four years to write the thirteenth amendment, and the red ink in which it was written cost many million dollars. It required 2000 years and many millions of men, to write that first amendment. Who can enumerate the cost or estimate the sacrifice? What vision at one sweep can take in the scope of its history? It reaches from the public ministry of Christ to the first term of Washington's administration. The panorama rapidly passing its shifting scenes before the public gaze, reveals strangely varied and bloody scenes of persecution. In one blurred vision the commingled raging of the Numidian lion on the Roman amphitheatre, the rack and dungeon of the Inquisition, the autodafes and bonfires with human victims, confiscation of property and toil through long, dark ages, tell the story.

Under the head of remote history one cannot well confine investigation to less than six inquiries:

First. What theories and practices concerning the relation of religion and state were prevalent throughout the Old World prior to the adoption of this amendment?

Second. How far persecution on account of religion by the governments of the Old World had constrained the settlement of the colonies, and particularly how far the persecuted exiles were led by their own wrongs in the direction of this amendment?

Third. How far religious persecution by any older colony influenced the establishment of a new one, and how far such treatment prepared the new colony for this amendment?

Fourth. What was the established relation of church and state in each colony while under colonial patents, grants, charters or direct rule of the crown, and what the trend on the minds of the people resulting from the historical lessons of this relation?

Fifth. What progress towards this amendment is indicated in the Declaration of Independence and subsequent articles of Confederation?

Sixth. What modifications in the same direction are disclosed by such state constitutions as were adopted by the people after renouncing allegiance to England, and prior to the adoption of this amendment?

One should be far from saying that these six are all the important inquiries pertinent to the remote history of this amendment, but may well claim that these inquiries at least must be intelligently answered by any student who assumes preliminary knowledge of the subject. Nature has no leaps, nor has history. It records developments. The education necessary to the adoption of this amendment was as slow, gradual and costly as any other grinding of the mills of the gods. Time allows but a statement of these questions, with briefest answers to some.

All past theories on the relation of religion and state which had found embodiment in law, are reducible to these two: First. Whose is the state, his is the religion. Second. Whose is the religion, his is the state. You will observe that both prescribe union of church and state. In the first the state is on top regulating religion. In the second the church is on top regulating the state.

Pagan Rome illustrates the first, with Julius Caesar as pontifex maximus. Papal Rome illustrates the second, with G r e g o r y the Great as pontiff. In either case the election to office accords with its theory. A political election inducts Caesar into his religious office; the state must regulate religion. A religious election inducts Gregory the Great into his pontificate of authority over all states; religion must regulate the state.

But papal and pagan Rome do not exhaust the illustration. All other lands and all Protestant governments illustrate one or the other theory just as well. Germany, England, Switzerland, Scotland, Holland and the Scandinavian states, all Protestant, firmly held to one or the other of these theories. Just when one is disposed to place John Calvin on the pinnacle of intellectual religious fame, he is repelled by the smell of the burning of Cervetus. Luther, Zwingle, Melanchthon, Maurice of Orange, John Knox and Latimer, all were persecutors, all opposed to religious liberty.

It sickens and saddens the mind to see how little effect persecution had on the persecuted, to lead them in the direction of even toleration. No matter whether the persecutor or persecuted was Protestant or papist.

In my own ancestry there is ample illustration. My maternal ancestor was a Huguenot exile, driven by the revocation of the Edict of Nantes to South Carolina in 1690. My paternal ancestors suffered as Romanists under the persecution of the established church in Ireland long before they became Baptists.

With what elation of the heart does the student of history read the glorious defence by pike and dike against the Spaniards made by the Dutch Calvinists, but how sad to see these same intolerant Calvinists through the hero, Prince Maurice, arrest and behead John van Olden Barneveldt, who was really the saviour of his country, and by far the greatest statesman of his generation.

Who does not shudder at the imprisonment of the grandest scholar of his time, Grotius, because he held to the five points of Arminianism, in contradistinction to the five points of Calvanism, but yet if I were to-day to recite in the hearing of you young people, the five original points of Arminianism, as drafted by Arminius himself, and not as Arminianism as gone to seed in modern Wesleyism, one half of you perhaps would swallow them whole without dissent.

But Henry the Eighth, in establishing Episcopacy, did not give religious freedom to his people. He only claimed for himself the place of the Pope. Whose is the state, his is the religion. And after him for quite a while as Romanist or Protestant ascended the throne, each monarch re-echoed: mine is the state and mine is the religion. Neither the house of Tudor nor the Stuarts knew anything of even genuine toleration, much less religious liberty.

Persecution for conscience' sake raged throughout the Romanist and Protestant world; hence persecution led to the settlement of the colonies of America. They were exiles for conscience' sake. Here the Protestant in power exiled the Romanist; there the Romanist with rack, dungeon and stake, exiled the Protestant. But the exiles, setting up for themselves on new shores, whether Protestant or Romanist, denied to others what they claimed for themselves. These colonists, I repeat, driven themselves by persecution to find a home in a new world, hesitated not by persecution to drive away dissenters, thus influencing the establishment of other colonies. Persecution in Virginia under the establishment of the church of England, led to the settlement of the Carolinas. Persecution in Massachusetts led to the settlement in Rhode Island and Pennsylvania.

Spread the map of the world before you and look at its zones. On all this plane there was only one little spot of earth seen by the sun in his circuit devoted to religious liberty. That spot was Rhode Island. Notwithstanding the claims that have been made in behalf of Maryland, here in Baltimore, I dare to say it, that in Rhode Island alone of all the world from the creation of Adam down to the adoption of this amendment there was and had been only one government that allowed to all its people true soul liberty. The claim of Maryland is absolutely untenable. True there was toleration, but even in the best days of toleration, the statute book held the penalty of death and confiscation for any man who dared to revile the Virgin Mary.

We find but little brighter light even in the state Constitutions adopted during the Revolutionary War. Seven of the Constitutions had some religious test of office. In three of them preachers of the gospel were ineligible to office. In four of them the Romanist was ineligible; and in nine of them the Jew, the kinsman of Christ, was ineligible to office.

As a sample of religious persecution by the state, suppose some of you young people ask the representatives of the Publication Society here to let you have the history of the Philadelphia Baptist Association for one hundred years, from 1707 to 1807; then turn to the 115th page and read the remarkable letters from New England to that Association in 1770, concerning the sufferings of our Baptist brethren in Connecticut. What a thrilling story of American history.

Here at Ashfield, a large Baptist settlement, with only five pedo-Baptist families in it, were compelled by law to build a house of worship for the Presbyterians, and pay for the support of the Presbyterian minister. The best part of their orchards and farms were sold, were knocked down by forced sales under the sheriff's hammer at a ruinous price, to their persecutors. Property worth 365 pounds sterling was sold for 35 pounds. This only as a first payment. When they complained, their comfort was this answer: "The General Assembly had a right to do what they did, and if you do not like it you may quit this place," while a Mr. Wells stood up to preach a mock sermon for their consolation, saying words to this effect: "The Baptists, for refusing to pay an orthodox minister shall be cut in pound pieces and boiled for their fat to grease the Devil's carriage."

But as the details are too multitudinous for special reference, let us for illustration cite the cases of Massachusetts and Virginia. Massachusetts was settled by the Pilgrim fathers landing at Plymouth Rock, December 30, 1620. A second colony at Massachusetts bay in 1629. The two were united under one charter in 1692. The state Constitution was adopted in 1780, though afterwards amended.

Massachusetts in its government, as determined on ship-board before landing, was a Simon pure theocracy, and the living embodiment of the theory, whose is the religion, his is the state. The doctrine of the theocray was no more tolerant as coming from their lips than from the lips of the Pope of Rome. If you would find embodied in a few words that doctrine, turn to Bancroft's History of the United States, revised edition, volume I, pages 449-461. In 1629 they exiled Episcopacy in the person of the Browns. In 1636 they exiled Roger Williams; in 1651 they fined Clark and mercilessly whipped Holmes, our Baptist sires. From 1656 to 1658 they put Quakers to death or in prison, or drove them into exile. In 1662 they established censorship of the press and persecuted all dissenters. From 1689 to 1692 they hanged, jailed, and tortured witches.

In no Constitution adopted during the Revolutionary war, is there such a thing as religious liberty. And in the debate on the adoption of the Federal Constitution, by the Massachusetts convention, a prominent member urged as a specific objection that it had no religious test, to be answered by our Baptist sire, Isaac Backus, that the absence of that test constituted its glory and recommendation. It is quite an interesting study, in comparing the several Constitutions in the states as adopted or amended at different times, to trace the development of the true religious idea in the "whereas" and "although."

The Constitution of Massachusetts in its section on religion, commences substantially, "whereas piety and good morals are essential to good government, therefore the state may require, etc." Later Constitutions referring to the same fact, deduce different conclusions, to wit: "Although piety and good morals are necessary to good government yet the state has no authority to regulate religion."

Virginia was as bad as Massachusetts. I have not time to tell the story. When Lord Baltimore landed there they presented an iron-clad oath they knew no Romanist could take, and so he turned toward Maryland. Others they drove to the Carolinas. Read in Semple's history, in the papers of Madison and Jefferson, how arduous was the struggle for the disestablishment of the church of England and the securing to all of the people full, free religious liberty.

I repeat the statement that the history of this first amendment is complex in root, stem and branch. The Constitution was submitted to thirteen different conventions, preceded by thirteen distinct canvasses. In no two states was the canvass the same. The immediate occasion of the adoption of the first ten amendments is cited in their preamble, substantially to wit: While all the state conventions had unconditionally ratified the Constitution as submitted, yet many of them had urged and recommended certain amendments, more explicitly guarding the rights of the constituent states and the individual from possible federal tyranny, without a reasonable hope of obtaining which, ratification could not have been secured.

Mark the fact that in the constitutional convention itself the incorporation of a Bill of Rights had been voted down. To the absence of this bill of rights the old continental congress had objected, but had no power to make additions to the instrument. A number of the state legislatures had also objected, and were equally without power to incorporate their objections, but at last, as has been stated, the Bill of Rights became a part of the organic law of the land. It is an interesting study to note the trend of subsequent federal enactments. I would ask you young people, in this direction, to note particularly the remarkable treaty with Tripoli, negotiated by Joel Barlow under appointment from Washington, and ratified in the first term of Adam's administration. That treaty used this express language, "The government of the United States is in no sense founded on the Christian religion."

Note also in this connection the remarkable report of the committee to which was referred petitions concerning violation of the Sunday law under operations of the postal laws. This report, presented by R. M. Johnson, of Kentucky, is indeed one of the most remarkable documents on the relation of the church and state in the annals of time. Then notice the defeat of the Blair Bills, and the reasons assigned for their rejection by the United States Congress. I refer to the Sunday Rest Bill and the Education Bill.

But I would have you to particularly notice the language and force of this first amendment. Mark you — it says: "Congress shall make no law respecting the establishment of religion or prohibiting the free exercise thereof." Congress, that means that the central government shall not oppress or discriminate in religious matters. It is no guarantee whatever against state oppression, for as a matter of fact long subsequent to the adoption of this amendment under state laws there have been religious discriminations and oppressions. Some of these discriminating statutes remained unexpunged until a period within the memory of men now living, and to-day this amendment does not guarantee any of you young people from religious oppression by any state in this union.

There remain yet unsettled great questions of vital interest to which only the briefest reference without discussion can be made. I have never yet found a man whose own mind was fully settled upon all of them. To wit: The Bible in the public school, Sunday laws, and taxes upon church houses. Earth has no wisdom far-reaching enough to forecast the final result upon these kindred topics.

My own views upon all of them I could give you, if I had the time, but there remain but a few minutes of my time, in which, in briefest generalizations I now address myself to the last part of my subject: The part performed by our Baptist fathers in the adoption of this first amendment. It is too hot for declamation or for sober historic investigation. You are too crowded and uncomfortable, and all the conditions are favorable only to pop gun talks and not to grave historical investigations; therefore I must content myself with a few simple affirmations embodying all in this one proposition: Had there been no Baptists there had been no first amendment.

I hold myself responsible to maintain the truth of this proposition, and count myself able on occasion to trace through hundreds of years of history the educational development which led to this amendment in the history of our Baptist fathers. The principles and polity alone fit the amendment as a substratum. Their sufferings best illustrate its necessity. Their memorials to governments and governmental officials furnish the true arguments for its adoption. Their refusal under any circumstances to accept state aid in fostering religion is unique in history.

In Holland, though forced by law to assist in the payment of the ministry of other denominations, they refused state aid for themselves; and well do I remember some years since, when as one of a committee appointed by the Southern Baptist Convention to consider the propriety of accepting property worth $250,000 tendered to us by the Mexican states, Nueva Leon and Coahuila, on condition that we would establish schools thereon, we unanimously rejected the free gift of this vast property because opposed to Baptist principles, and bought it rather and established our schools.

In the addresses delivered during the Centennial year, particularly those by Drs. J. L. M. Curry and G. B. Taylor, and in the histories of Semple, Peck, Cramp, Backus, Jones, Curtis, Armitage and of other Baptist historians, and in more recent publications by the Knolys Society in London, are made known the details of the Baptist struggle.

Let me say to you young people that our Baptist history and name are not without spots. As a people we have grievous faults, much to be deplored, but all things considered, to them far more than to any other people on this earth, belongs the trophy of both civil and religious liberty — of genuine soul liberty.

For one, I glory in the record they have made. I feel a responsibility resting upon me to transmit, unimpaired, as far as lies in my power, the glorious heritage they bequeathed to those who shall come after me. There is no need to blush for the record of your sires. Take care that your sires blush not for the record of their sons and daughters. Take care that their principles and policy, their simplicity and purity of doctrine be not diluted or rendered degenerate, as illustrated in your life and teachings.

They have emerged from the clouds, the mists and the shadows. Their fellowship once despised is now sought on all hands. They are here ten thousand strong. I expect, God helping them, that they will be everywhere. That Providence which has brought them through the fires of persecution and from lone wanderings in exile and crowned them with the glories of triumph will not, I trust, allow them to lose their pristine devotion to God and the rights of man.

Dark indeed will be the day when their principles wax cold and their policy enfeebles; sad will be the day for mankind when the purity of their doctrine and the simplicity of their worship is marred by a return to ritualism, or to any form of sacramental salvation. They alone are entitled under God to full praise for offering to the world the Bible in its true rendering, unshadowed by any priest. They alone will not allow intervention between the individual and his God, not even the baptismal pool.

I can not forbear to warn you young people that the grey-headed men now about to pass away have some failings of heart lest you younger people shall not preserve the principles they have cherished as dearer than life. Whenever you turn from them, whenever you dilute them, whenever you put a society above the church, that pillar and ground of the truth, whenever you tend toward superstitions of the past, or the latitudinarianism of the present, then may the organization of the Baptist Young People's Union perish from the face of the earth. But in so far as you faithfully walk in the well trodden paths of your fathers, that far may the smiles of God brighten your pathway, and the approbation of God crown your efforts.

V

PROHIBITION NOT A PARTY FIGHT

—oOo—

WHAT THE GREAT DEMOCRATIC
LEADERS SAY

(An address to the people of Texas, Waco, Texas, 1887.)

The Prohibition State Central Committee desires to restate for the information of all the people in Texas the following fundamental principles in the present campaign:

1. Our Committee was created and commissioned by a non-partisan, non-political convention.

2. The instructions of that convention imperatively require us to conduct this campaign *as citizens of Texas* without regard to partisan politics or religious alignments, or emoluments in office.

3. Our purpose to implicitly obey these instructions has been published to the world and is hereby reaffirmed.

4. But notwithstanding the a c t i o n of our Legislature in dissociating this election from all others and from any candidacy for office that the people of Texas as citizens might determine the propriety and expediency of this police regulation upon its intrinsic merits, an effort has been made and is still being made to obtrude extraneous and irrelevant issues into the canvass and to inject into it partisan politics with a view to complicate and mystify a simple proposition, so as to thereby defeat an impartial and dispassionate consideration of the subject.

To particularize: We have been challenged by the chairman of the Anti-Prohibition Convention to enter a theological controversy. Labored efforts have been put forth to align against the amendment the Democratic party as a party. It is true such efforts have signally failed. But that this matter may be put finally to rest and that the people may, for themselves and upon their individual convictions vote upon this amendment according to its merits and without fear of incurring the charge of disloyalty to their party we submit the following facts and declarations:

FACTS

1. The opening speeches of the campaign for and against prohibition were delivered on the same occasion and before the same audience by the Hon. Barnett Gibbs, and Arch Cochran, the former a Democratic contestant for Congressman Olin Wilborn's seat and the latter the Republican candidate for governor, defeated by General Ross, the Democratic nominee. If prohibition is designed to break up the Democratic party then Dr. Arch Cochran is a leader of the wrong post; and if it is designed to break up the Republican party then Mr. Gibbs is on the wrong side. But as a demonstration that the issue is non-partisan, these two irreconcilable political opponents gave each other the hand of fellowship, *on this matter*, before all the people.

2. In his zealous efforts to organize the opposition to Prohibition, Mr. Gibbs summoned, by telegram, the Hon. Exall, Chairman of the Democratic State Executive Committee, to a consultation in Austin. Mr. Exall, with his characteristic discretion and sound wisdom, declined to sign his name to a call for an Anti-Prohibition Convention on the just ground that such action on his part might be construed to imply that the Democratic party, as a party, was committed against prohibition, which in his judgment, was contrary to the official and authoritative expression of that party in its last State Convention.

3. The correctness of Col. Exall's judgment of the import of that decision of the Democratic State Convention is confirmed by this explicit declaration of Senator Richard Coke, in his recent open letter to the Dallas Herald.

4. Any effort to escape this interpretation of the party platform, based upon an assumed and fictitious distinction, so far as principle is concerned, between Local option and State Prohibition is defeated by the following published declaration of Congressman Mills and of Senator Coke, and is also defeated by the well-known fact that the Democratic Legislature which, upon the recommendation of Gov. Ross, submitted this amendment, refused to entertain a proposition to order this election at the same time of the general election.

5. That this refusal was based upon their desire to separate this issue from party politics is manifest by the following declaration signed by Democratic members of that legislature.

All these impregnable facts, which are only a few of the many which could be submitted are supported by the following explicit and categorical answers to questions propounded by our committee.

Now in view of these facts and declarations are we not justified in asking the people to rebuke the attempt of a few politicians who seek to thwart the wishes of the Legislature and of the people by embittering this controversy with partisan politics, and by their more reprehensible action in projecting a so-called *religious* platform, and attempting to inaugurate a religious crusade?

We therefore, confidently appeal to the people of Texas without regard to party politics, or religious views to unite with us as citizens of Texas in abolishing *Union between whisky and the state* as the great Jefferson, James Madison, Patrick Henry and men of all religious denominations, united to divorce the unholy alliance of church and state.

We do not believe that either one, however good or bad should have such connection. We call upon you, fellow citizens, to aid in purifying the ballot box, the police courts, the legislature, and all municipal and state governments from the polluting influence of the saloons and to eliminate from the body politic that dominating and overshadowing monopoly which to-day darkens every hearthstone, menaces every free institution, and defiantly violates every law.

We ask you, as a people, to rise up in your majesty and redeem the land from the terrible waste of material resources, that undermining power which saps the foundations of all social purity, that *Organized Plutocracy* which is even ready to import its millions from Northern breweries and distilleries into Texas, to buy up, browbeat, and dominate a free Texas Election. We ask you, you who have ever resisted invasion from foreign shores, if you will allow this corrupting tide of money, poured out from inexhaustible coffers, ever filling with the price of slaves and the souls of men, to defeat the will of the people.

We do not mean and do not affirm that the Democratic party, as a party is committed to prohibition but we do mean and affirm that as a party it is not only not committed against prohibition (for even its silence would prove that much) but that it is committed to the doctrine that this is a non-partisan question, and therefore that Democrats, as citizens, may vote for or against prohibition without forfeiting party affiliation, and without diminution of party fealty and allegiance. Hence our position is that no Democrat should receive party condenmnation for expressing and voting his convictions on either side of this question.

But if any Democrat, whether prohibitionist or anti-prohibitionist, shall attempt to coerce by invoking the party name, his brother Democrat who differs from him upon this non-partisan question, such a man should be held and treated now and hereafter *as a bolter* from his party platform and being thereby a disorganizer, should be excommunicated from the Democratic party.

VI

A LITTLE MORE GRAPE
(An open letter on domestic wines in Texas.)

—oOo—

Dr. Carroll's Views on Grape Culture:
An Industry That will Not be Affected
by Prohibition.

Waco, Tex., May 11, 1887.

Messrs. Bullock, Fuller and Carswell,
Decatur, Texas.

Gentlemen: — Your favor of yesterday just received and the contents noted. The statement contained that you are prohibitionists and that you favor the proposed constitutional amendment in its present form is gratifying to our Central committee.

It is strictly true, as you suggest, that if native wines and beer had been exempted, the opposition would have found more "bugs under the chip" than in the present form of the bill. Judge Terrell's speech in 1881 sufficiently proves that.

But you call attention to the fact that Wise county is largely given to grape culture, there being, as you allege, five *acres in all* so devoted, which produces *annually* the enormous amount of *twenty barrels of domestic wine*. That this immense business is controlled by a few Germans. And then you ask how best to meet an anti-prohibition objection thus stated: "Under the proposed amendment these half a dozen Germans could not make their own wine from their own grapes, but might import foreign wines for their tables, thus discriminating against Texas products and in favor of foreign products." I believe this is a fair statement of the case and its difficulties.

Under the pressure of much business, I send you off-hand the following reply, and as others over the state may be propounding similar questions, you will excuse me for making the reply in this public form:

1. My immediate neighbor, Colonel J. M. Anderson, one of the ablest and most zealous prohibitionists in Texas, has a vineyard in which all the Wise county vineyards could be dropped and lost. He, though his money is invested in this way, and though he is a sharp business man, sees no trouble, financial or otherwise, threatened by this amendment against his present grape-culture or the indefinite extension of the business. On the contrary he expects to derive great benefit to grape culture by the adoption of the amendment. Even one well-ascertained fact is worth much. If it be good for him it can be made good for the other grape-culturists in Texas. And why? Because under the restrictions of this amendment grape-culture in Texas can be made enormously profitable. Texas pays annually a vast sum of money for raisins and canned grapes, which are all imported goods. Why cannot our home market vineyards supply this immense market? If our state is adapted by nature to this industry, then here is an open and unoccupied field which will call for increase in the extent and yield of our vineyards ten thousand fold.

2. If it is preferred to convert these grapes into wine, then there are more processes than one, well known for 4000 years by which an utterly unintoxicating wine can be made, which is delightful to the palate, nourishing as a food, and every way preferable to fermented and intoxicating wines. By cooling processes, or by boiling, a sweet and delicious wine can be made, which will keep pure, which will be a valuable commodity. A vineyard so devoted will be lighted up by day by the radiant smiles of God and be bedewed at night with his benediction. "Thus

saith the Lord, As the new wine is found in the cluster, and one saith, Destroy it not; for a blessing is in it," Isa. 65:8.

That such wine can be made, that it can be preserved, and that it is wholesome, palatable and nutritious is the testimony of history. About such wine, Aristotle, Pliny, Virgil and many classical authors speak. This amendment, therefore, will not dig up a single grapevine in Texas.

It is frankly conceded, however, that the law will forbid the making of *intoxicating* wines, and justly so, because there is a curse in them.

3. Texas cannot prohibit the importation of liquors, because that matter is controlled by the laws of the United States Congress. The following unquestioned decision of the Supreme court settles that matter:

"Spirits and distilled liquors are universally admitted to be subjects of ownership and property; and are therefore subjects of exchange, bartar and traffic, like any other commodity in which a right of property exists; and inasmuch as the laws of Congress authorize the importation, no state has a right to prohibit their introduction. But although the importation cannot be prohibited by a state, the state is not bound to furnish a market for it, and may restrain or prohibit the sale after it is brought into the state." — 5th Howard's U. S. Rep. 577.

For such a product God sends His rains upon the earth that it may bring forth food. "And wine that maketh glad the heart of man, and oil to make his face to shine, and bread which strengtheneth man's heart," Psa. 104:15.

This "fruit of the vine" God by natural processes *makes out of the water* which falls from the skies. In the clouds he brews it and in the furrows he distills it. In the chemical laboratory of nature, by slow, natural processes he ordinarily converts this water into wine. Once only, by instantaneous miracle, without fermentation or distillation, but by omnific will, "He looked upon the water — and the conscious water saw its God and blushed."

But discrimination against Texas products does not follow from this decision. As soon as the imports cross our boundary line they become immediately subject to the prohibition law. They *cannot be sold.* All experience proves that when you enforce the law against the sale, you practically and virtually break up the importation to any harmful extent. Because the foreign manufacturers of malt, vinous and spirituous liquors KNOW this they therefore expend millions in desperate attempts to defeat prohibition.

4. Under existing conditions, grape culture in Texas is infinitesimal, and will remain so while these conditions last. Hence there is perhaps not a nickel contributed by this business to defeat this amendment. Texas home products is not making this fight. It was not a convention of Pecos grape growers that issued that secret circular rebuking a Texas legislature and marking out a plan of campaign and furnishing "the images of Augustus" therefor. No! It was an outside and foreign brewery. Our fight is not against native grapes but against foreign distillers of sour mash.

These outside syndicates well know that with the start they have, and the capital invested, and their compact organization THEY CAN KEEP DOWN *Texas products forever,* unless prohibition prevails. They also well know that if this amendment passes, it will, by refusing sale, practically exclude foreign products and *give Texas vineyards a chance for development,* which can never be done while they, by powerful concentration of capital, monopolize the business.

I give it as my deliberate judgment that under the existing conditions, Texas grape culture will never have a chance to appreciably develop. That the home industry will be stifled and throttled by all-powerful outside competition.

It is also my deliberate conviction that under the workings of this amendment Texas vineyards may be lawfully multiplied tenfold every year. Let our grapes be converted, by cooling or boiling process, into UNFERMENTED, UNINTOXICATING wines, and they may be placed, without offense to law or harm to consumers, on every man's table in Texas. The very children can take "such wine with their milk."

5. But if you exempt from prohibition native wines and beer, i.e., intoxicating wine and beer, you must also exempt the same articles from abroad. You cannot under the constitution allow Texas products to be sold and deny a sale to outside products. This being true, Texas vineyards could never be developed. California alone would by its overwhelming competition choke off the increase of Texas grape culture.

And as for beer, in order to satisfy yourself spend one day each in Denison and Texarkana, watching incoming freight trains. You will see as many as THREE BEER TRAINS a day rolling in. An Arkansas man who had wearied himself of Texarkana, counting these trains asked one of our citizens: "Do all you fellows in Texas drink beer? Do you ever drink any water?" Such a sight once seen will open your eyes about any chance to develop Texas products under existing conditions. The very cars as they rattle in have settled into a patent tune as follows: "Anheuser — Sour Mash — Budweiser! Budweiser — Sour Mash — Anheuser! Anheuser — Budweiser — Sour Mash."

Respectfully,
B. H. Carroll

VII

THE LIQUOR TRAFFIC

—oOo—

ITS RELATIONS TO THE LAW AND TO SOCIETY

—oOo—

*It May be Regulated or Repressed Without
an Evasion of Liberty — Dr. Carroll's Masterly Speech at
Padgitt's Park.*

—oOo—

UNFAIR TERMS OF DISCUSSION

FELLOW CITIZENS: I have never heard the Hon.
R. Q. Mills make a speech, on any subject, in my
life. To-day, at his own appointment, I am required
by the only attainable terms of discussion, to reply,
beforehand, to the speech he will make when I am
done. It will not do to say that I have a half hour's
rejoinder, because that half hour must be used, according to the same anti-Prohibition formula, in re-
plying, again beforehand, to his closing speech.

Nor will it avail to say that I am in the affirm-
ative, for in that case, according to all accepted
rules of debate, I would have the closing speech.
The challenge for this discussion came primarily
from Judge Clark, who claimed and dictated every
term of the discussion, whether of time, order or
place.

Being unable to corkscrew any other terms out
of him, I have recalled my published appointments
at Will's Point and Tyler to meet this Ajax Telamon
of the liquor traffic on any terms.

A few days ago I met his lieutenants, John D.

Lee and Rufus Hardy, at Athens. Not having gone as far into this matter as their chieftain, they accepted fair and honorable terms of discussion, and fought their battle out manfully.

While I have instructed my boys never to exact an advantage of an adversary while they bear my name, yet for myself I rejoice to grapple with Col. Mills on unequal terms because it lays the foundation for his argument.

If such a man as Congressman Mills, a redoubtful athlete and oiled gladiator on a hundred arenas, State and national, requires manifest advantages in meeting one whom he is pleased to style " a political priest," then the conclusion comes like a conquerer that a conscious weakness of a bad cause claims unusual favors, unknown, undemanded and unaccorded in righteous controversies.

That bad cause it is now my pleasure and duty to impeach of high crimes and misdemeanors. After drawing my bow at a venture, and a shaft where I suppose my adversary to be I must then stand uncovered, in an open field and receive the hot shot where he knows me to be.

Concerning Col. Mill's private character or personal habits, either past or present, I have nothing to say, except to concede cheerfully in that direction all that he himself or his warmest admirers may claim. With measures, and not personalities, is my business to-day.

In this connection it affords me pleasure to say here and now, that on this subject the right of private judgment ought to be ungrudgingly accorded to all men, whether white or black, saint or sinner. Precedent to all argument I desire here to read certain

GREAT PRINCIPLES

enunciated by Thomas Jefferson, S. J. Tilden, John Stuart Mill and Victor Hugo. Three of the quotations from Jefferson and one from Mr. Tilden are taken from Col. Mill's speech at Corsicana which was handed me yesterday evening.

Mr. Jefferson says: "It is better to keep the wolf out of the fold than to turn to drawing his teeth and talons after he shall have entered." Vol. VIII, page 398. Again as quoted on the twelfth page of Mr. Mill's speech: "In questions of power," he says to us, "let no more be heard of confidence in man but bind him down from mischief by the claims of the Constitution."

Again on the 16th page of the speech quoted from Mr. Jefferson's inaugural address: "With all these blessings what more is necessary to make us a happy and prosperous people? Still one thing more, fellow citizens, a wise and frugal government, which shall restrain men from injuring one another, which shall leave them otherwise free to regulate their own pursuits of industry and improvement and shall not take from the mouth of labor the bread it has earned. This is the sum of good government and this is necessary to close the circles of our felicities."

Jefferson Memoirs, Vol. 1, pages 66, 67: "Honest error must be arrested where its toleration leads to public ruin — as, for the safety of society, we commit honest maniacs to Bedlam, so judges should be withdrawn from their bench whose erroneous biases are leading us to dissolution. I may indeed injure them in fame or fortune, but it saves the republic which is the first and supreme law."

LETTER TO JOHN TAYLOR

May 28, 1816.

"Believing as I do, that the mass of the citizens is the safest depository of their own rights, and especially that the evils flowing from the duperies of the people are less injurious than those from the egotism of the agents, I am a friend to that composition of government which has in it the most of this ingredient."

S. J. Tilden as quoted by Roger Q. Mills: "In a free country the curtailment of the absolute rights of the individual should only be such as is essential to the peace and good order of the community."

WHAT MR. JOHN STUART MILLS SAYS AS TO THE PRINCIPLES INVOLVED

On the 20th page, after stating the object of his essay to be the assertion of one simple principle, he thus defines the principle: "That principle is, that the sole end for which mankind are warranted, individually or collectively, in interfering with the liberty of action of any of their number, is selfprotection. That the only purpose for which power can be rightfully exercised over any member of a civilized community against his will is to prevent harm to others."

On the 125th page where he is endeavoring to ascertain the rightful limit to the sovereignty of the individual and just where the authority of society commences, he says: "To individuality should belong the part of life in which it is chiefly the individual that is interested; to society the part which chiefly interests society."

On the next page he adds: "As soon as any part of a person's conduct affects prejudicially the interests of others, society has jurisdiction over it, and the question whether the general welfare will or will not be promoted by interfering with it, becomes an open question."

On the 123rd page, after discussing some individual action which society should not touch, he adds: "It is far otherwise if he has infringed the rules necessary for the protection of his fellow creatures individually or collectively. The evil consequences of his acts do not then fall on himself, but on others; and society as the protector of all its members, must retaliate on him; must inflict pain on him for the express purpose of punishment, and must take care that it be sufficiently severe."

On the 137th page he sums up the matter thus: "Whenever, in short, there is a definite damage, or a definite risk of damage, either to a individual or to the public, the case is taken out of the province of liberty, and placed in that of morality of laws."

On the 158th page he continues: "Trade is a social act. Whoever undertakes to sell any description of goods to the public, does what affects the interest of other persons, and of society in general; and thus his conduct, in principle, comes within the jurisdiction of society."

Victor Hugo says: "The French convention promulgated this great axiom: 'The liberty of each citizen ends where the liberty of another commences,' which comprises in two lines all human, social law."

Let us now consider the

APPLICATION OF THESE PRINCIPLES

to the question under discussion. As Col. Mills quotes the most of them, and doubtless approves them all, they constitute his major proposition on personal liberty as applied to the proposed amendment. To avail himself anything in this discussion, his major proposition must logically be: The liquor traffic to be abolished by the Amendment does not injure society nor interfere with the peace and order of good Government. Strange as it may appear, he has never been known to address himself to the last proposition. He has been content to indulge in glittering generalities about personal liberty.

I press upon him to-day to redeem himself as a logician and statesman, by furnishing that proof of his, the second proposition which alone will entitle him to the benefit of the first. Let us consider

THE REAL QUESTION AT ISSUE.

I will state it plainly. There is now in our organic law a provision of the Constitution restricting the liquor traffic, at the option of any precinct, city or county in Texas. This Amendment merely proposes to enlarge and extend that restriction by State option.

The identity of local option, now in the Constitution, and the State option sought by this Amendment, I will now prove by the highest anti-Prohibition standards.

Senator Coke says: "Prohibition, or local option, cannot be maintained in the precinct, by any argument which is not equally potent to maintain it in the county and in the State, and vice versa. . . The argument would seem stronger for the county, and still stronger for the State: because of increased number, and therefore greater good. If good for the precinct, it is better for the county and best for the State." Interview in Galveston News, September, 1885.

This substantially he reiterates in strong language in his recently published letters. The Waco Examiner, the official organ of the anti-Prohibition Central committee and published under Judge Clark's own eye, under date of June 2, 1887, expresses agreement with Senator Coke and then calls "State Prohibition the logical conclusion of local option," and adds:

"If the state has no right to enforce Prohibition in counties which do not want it, by the same rule counties have no right to enforce it in precincts which do not want it, and of course it follows clearly and logically, that precincts have no right to enforce it on an individual who does not want it. This is the whole question in a nutshell."

My distinguished opponent, himself, in an interview, in the News, in 1885, substantially concurs as I remember, thus: "Local option is State Prohibition in spots."

Now upon this established identity between local option and State Prohibition, as to the principle involved, I here press upon Colonel Mills the following question: When was local option incorporated in our Constitution and who put it there? Will Col. Mills answer plainly and unequivocally?

Having thus indicated the principles involved, stated the question fairly, I now desire to introduce evidence that the liquor traffic is bad and not good; that it does injure society; that it does hurtfully disturb the peace and good order of government.

That my opponent may have fair opportunity to reply, I submit, in order, the following

INDICTMENT OF THE LIQUOR TRAFFIC:

1. In its present form we have an unhallowed union of whisky and the State.

This union is hurtful to the State and should be abolished. The State, therefore, becomes a partner in crime and virtually sells indulgences to commit crime.

Mr. Jefferson, in speaking of what he regarded as innocent lotteries, says: "This then is a declaration by the nation, that an act was not immoral, of which they were in the habitual use themselves as a part of the regular means of supporting the government. The tax on the vendor of the tickets, was their share of the profits, and if their share was innocent, his could not be criminal."

Every word of this is applicable to the liquor traffic. And, as John Leland, and others of my denominational sires, aided Jefferson, Patrick Henry and Madison, in abolishing the unholy union of Church and State, so now I rejoice to aid political leaders of my day in abolishing the equally unholy union of Whisky and State.

Will Mr. Mills say the liquor traffic is good? If it is bad, will he affirm that it is a fit subject of revenue? Senator Vest, of Missouri, his co-laborer at Washington, the great anti-Prohibition champion of this continent, says on the first page of his speech at Booneville, September, 1882: "If, to-day, by word or act of mine, I could obliterate the last vestige of the liquor traffic from the face of the earth, I would do it, so help me God, without one moment's reflection or meditation." Then let such a traffic be divorced from the State.

2. The liquor traffic conspires against a free ballot and a pure election. Fellow citizens, the ballot box is the very foundation of our government, and whatever digs up that foundation or debauches the voter is high treason against every principle of liberty and government. This, the liquor traffic does in every election, where even remotely its interests are involved. No fact of history is more widely known. Its evil and over-shadowing influence in this direction increase day by day and year by year. No thoughtful, no true patriot can look on with unconcern when witnessing its appalling power and alarming domination in this direction. We felt its terrible force in our little county local option election. Rockwall felt it a few days ago when extraneous funds and agencies conspired to rob a local community of the right of self-government. What county in Texas to-day can settle local option for itself without the intrusion and invasion of foreign men and money?

The Waco Examiner, Judge Clark's organ, has already announced the doom of local option. The most desperate fight is now being made in every local option county by the liquor men and their anti-Prohibition agents. If the ballot box is lost, all is lost, and yet this traffic is a standing menace against its purity.

3. The liquor traffic conspires against every municipality. It controls city governments. It dictates mayor, aldermen and police. This unrighteous domination becomes more formidable when you consider the debt of municipalities. Let all thoughtful

men hear me on this point. It is a fact of history, that the policy, home and foreign, of all governments is largely controlled by their bonded debt. These debts make peace or declare war. Well, then, the debts of our municipalities, our cities and towns, are larger in the aggregate, than the combined debts of the States and of the national government. When, then, the saloons control the cities, they wield the mighty power of these debts and as these debts dictate the policy of government they practically prescribe the policy of the whole United States. Look at San Antonio and other cities in Texas for example. Look and beware!

4. The liquor traffic conspires against every item of Mr. Jefferson's bill of rights. It interferes with freedom of religion. It places the freedom of the press between the upper and the nether millstone. Many a brave printer and editor has been thus ground to fine powder. It is a monstrous monopoly which overshadows our waters and darkens our land.

5. It creates a standing army of police which too often becomes their band of Myrmidons. For these the people pay. It makes, oftentimes, the right to trial by jury a farce. It sometimes stocks a Legislature by its still hunts. It lurks in the lobby, broods over the committee room and eats, drinks and sleeps with Legislators.

6. It perpetrates the most enormous crime on the colored people. These feeble folks, it debauches in every election. There is not a true man living who does not know that the best interests of the colored people would be subserved by the abolition of the liquor traffic. It keeps many of them homeless fugitives and renters. And yet their 80,000 votes in this election, conjoined with the foreign population, is the main hope for the perpetuity of the liquor traffic in Texas. I love these people. All my life I have lived among them. A dusky hand rocked my cradle. I hunted with them when a boy, by day and

by night — in southern swamps.

By their torchlight I spent many hours of the nights of my youth reading to them and teaching them. Every memory of the past reproduces their faces. It grieves me to see them the slaves of whisky and the football of whisky politicians. It is an awful and monstrous crime perpetrated by liquor men and their agents in debauching their ballot by exciting their fears of impossible dangers, concerning re-enslavement and the loss of their schools.

7. The liquor traffic dries up the true sources of revenue. Its greatest claim to life is the miserable pittance it pays into the public treasuries. I say miserable pittance in comparison with what it consumes, costs and destroys.

No man, in one short speech, can go into details on any special or present statistics worth hearing, without neglecting other lines of argument equally important. Leaving, therefore, statistics to the newspapers and pamphlets, I adopt for the present this shorter method. The liquor traffic dries up the sources of revenue in that it dissipates taxable values and destroys the brain power, industry and business capacity of producing taxable values.

To illustrate, A and B each own $10,000 worth of taxable values, each has the industry and business capacity of producing annually $3,000 worth of taxable values. C opens a saloon. A begins to drink and neglects his business. In the course of time his taxable values have melted away and his incapacity for business has destroyed his power to make other values. Then in a drunken row he commits a crime. What B pays into the public treasury is now diminished to furnish funds for prosecuting A. A expiates his offense on the gallows. His children inherit from him poverty and a bad name. Naturally this tends to make them Ishmaelites, with their hands against every man and every man's hand against them. They become worse criminals than A because their crime has become a profession from youth. Their children in turn follow them to the third and fourth generation. So that you never know when you get to the end of the taxation upon society growing out of C's saloon.

Finally upon this point, whatever may be the seeming force and plausible showing of tabulated statements about the increase of taxation resulting from the loss of revenue from the whisky traffic, all this conjecture, hypothesis and theory are annihilated by one rugged, granite, immovable fact, to wit:

Where Prohibition has been adopted, under anything like fair conditiions, it is a fact, that taxation has not increased in consequence of Prohibition. Take Atlanta. The official report of the officers of that city, at the close of the fiscal year 1886, after nine months' trial of Prohibition shows that

(1)   Taxes have not increased.

(2)   A cash balance of $41,000 more than the law requires is in the treasury.

(3)   They recommend a reduction of taxation.

(4)   They sold the 4½ per cent bonds at par in New York.

(5)   The facilities of their public schools, white and black, have been greatly enlarged and the attendance on both largely increased.

(6)   Better and more orderly classes of business have succeeded the expelled saloons.

(7)   The poor have been largely benefited by the morality enhanced.

The last biennial message of the governor of Kansas and the inaugural address of the governor of Maine both recommend a reduction of taxes and show material benefits arising from Prohibition. These facts, which outline themselves against the clear sky of human experience, overtop and outweigh a thousand plausible hypotheses predicated upon a facile array of statistics.

As a business proposition, considered merely from an economic standpoint, it is best for Texas to adopt this amendment. Our state is yet poor. We have but little money. Our name abroad, whether justly or unjustly, is bad. We are characterized as a people of train-robbers and hip-pocket pistols and rotten egg mobs. Capital is timid, immigration halts upon our borders.

Once flash the intelligence over the wires that Texas has redeemed herself from hoodlums and saloons and that our people will enforce the law, then will immigration pour in by the hundred thousand and eastern capital by the millions.

8. The liquor traffic, in this very campaign, has conspired against the Democracy of Texas. I speak advisedly. The conspiracy came to a head in the parlors of the Driskill hotel, in Austin, March 28th. To the outside world it was published that this fight would be outside of party lines and independent of the whisky men.

But Barnett Gibbs and others, appointed by Judge George Clark and others, by private letters, dated Austin, April 4, summoned such Democratic stalwarts as Maxey, Reagan, Culberson, Coke and others to meet in convention in Dallas, "to set forth plainly and unequivocally the time-honored principles of the Democratic party, from Thomas Jefferson down to the present time." There was no call for such a convention by the Democratic state Executive Committee. The purpose contemplated was contrary to the platform of the party adopted at Galveston.

It was contrary to the purpose of the Democratic Legislature which submitted the Amendment. And yet a vigorous effort was deliberately made to drag the Democratic party, as such, into this liquor trap. But on the 5th of April, Maxey, in reply to Mr. Gibbs exposed the fraud. His Democratic ear had never before heard the sound of such dark-lantern, u n d e r g r o u n d , know-nothing summons to battle. April 8th, John H. Reagan lifted the veil and exposed the bug under the chip. April

10th, Dave B. Culberson, our brainy Congressman from East Texas, denounced the whole thing as an organized revolt against the Democratic party. April 15th, our own great Senator, Richard Coke, raised his warning voice in protest and refused to be a party to the inquiry.

The boom of these four Democratic big guns echoed in the ears of the conspirators like the trump of judgment. The back-bone of the conspiracy was broken. These great men lifted the overwhelming clouds and flashed the calcium light of day upon these under-ground railroad sappers. My opponent, however, wrote a letter to Mr. Gibbs, approving the whole thing.

Well, they met in convention, perplexed by buzzing questions: How can we formulate Democratic doctrine? How can we break down such men as Reagan, Coke, Maxey, Culberson, Lanham, Miller, Wynne, Bonner and a host of others whose names were synonyms of Democracy? How can we formulate Democracy by the help of Melvin Wade and Dr. Arch Cochran? There in their committee, as I am informed, and on the trains afterwards, they cursed Coke with True Blue curses, and threatened to knife him.

All over the country and even here to-day the rumor flies, that they are grooming my opponent, Col. Mills, for the seat of our great Senator. If such be their purpose, let me assure them now, that no political racer, who was on that Dallas platform committee, and had a hand in formulating that piebald, ring-streaked and striped, Siamese twins, Jonas-faced p l a t f o r m can ever be successfully groomed to beat our great Senator. (Tremendous applause.)

After I exposed that platform in Belton, the Journal, then an anti-Prohibition paper, with brave honesty thus comments:

"How a thing can be un-Democratic and anti-Republican at the same time puzzles Dr. Carroll.

Well, we have wondered at that, too. The fact of the business is, a fauxpas was committed there. George Clark, in preparing the platform didn't write the words, 'and anti-Republican.' Mr. Mills, as Chairman of the committee on platform is responsible for those words being in the 'True Blue' platform."

Here to exculpate Judge Clark, the odium is placed on Col. Mills. Then to save Col. Mills, the Journal continues: "Every word of that platform was written by Hon. George Clark at his office, in Waco except two, and these were added at the request of Republican members of the convention."

Here we have it at last. It reminds me of a scene in the Garden of Eden. The Lord saying: "Adam, why did you eat that forbidden fruit?" Adam replies: "The woman thou gavest me, she tempted me and I did eat." The Lord then says: "Eve, why did you do this?" Eve replies: "The devil beguiled me and I did eat."

So when an outraged democracy shall ask: "Judge Clark, why did you eat this forbidden Republican fruit?" the judge makes the characteristic reply: "I deny it. I didn't do it. Col. Mills, the chairman of the True Blues, gave me; he tempted me, and I did eat." Then will the democracy say: "Col. Mills, why did you do this?" And the colonel replies: "Dr. Arch Cochran beguiled me and I did eat." Yes, fellow-citizen, Dr. Cochran is no fool; he scooped the whole lot of them in his little net.

Contrary to all their past utterances, and the slogan of their party, he made them give him a certificate, over their own signatures, that "paternalism is anti-Republican." He made them recant their allegation that Prohibition is a Republican trick. For all which in return, he certified that their democracy is all right! But who will take his certificate, though countersigned by Melvin Wade, as a good Democratic paper?

Thus ended the first scene of the great con-spiracy against Democracy. The curtain will rise on the next scene when Dr. Cochran meets these gentlemen at Phillipi in 1888, waving this very plat-form in their faces.

9. My last indictment against the traffic is that it has virtually robbed an admiring people of their brilliant congressman, R. Q. Mills. It has stolen him from the hearts of the pure and just, and made him the toast of the saloon and the song of the drunkard. It has converted his matchless genius, which like a soaring eagle, was flashing its pinions in the eye of the sun, into a low-flying raven which lights with ominous croak upon the bust of Liberty in every house, and throws its shadow on every floor, and digs its beak and talons in every heart, and appalls every soul with its doleful re-frain, "Nevermore."

It has made him bring up before the walled city of Democracy, a Trojan horse, branded on one side "Personal Liberty," and on the other a bunch of grapes. But when any Democratic Laocoon smites its hollow sides, and shows the glaring eyes of An-heuser and sour mash peeping from within, then the great python of the liquor traffic, crawls from its slimy sea, and wraps its anaconda folds around Laocoon, while the yelling mob, betrayed to death, shouts out: "A judgment of God."

Under the influence of this traffic, Col. Mills has been made to see each martyred wife and mother led to a fate worse than the guillotine, while like Madam Rolan, she turns her anguished eyes upon our once great Congressman, and says: "O Liberty, how many crimes are committed in thy name?" While just across the way the reeling drunkard, in maud-lin tones, is shouting: "Rah, for Col. Mills and liberty!"

It has made him pull down Bartholdi's statue of Liberty, enlightening the World with its silver light, and substitute a wrecker's beacon, whose lurid torch lures storm-tossed ships to disaster, plunder and death.

It has made him outlaw Columbia, the virgin daughter of the skies, and introduced the Mokanna of the liquor traffic, whose hideous deformities are masked in Lberty's stolen veil. He has transfixed the American Eagle, with an arrow feathered from its own wing, and substituted a brooding vampire which sucks the life-blood of the nation. See how it has converted a sturdy statesman into a political acrobat! In 1885 he sired Prohibition in Texas and now calls his thirty-two year-old boy "A Kansas Bantling."

Just look how ridiculous it makes him, trying to palm off his 32 year-old son as the bantling of a Kansas virgin only six years old! You might with more reason call Cain the father of Adam. And when the sturdy son refuses to be an orphan, and claims father in open court, the ungrateful father denounces his offspring as a "New England pirate — a corsair."

He says this Prohibition baby was spun "more than thirty years ago from the brain of the descendants of the Salem witch-burners." Well, just thirty-two years ago he claimed paternity of this child in Texas. What an autographic comment upon his own genealogy.

Again, in this same speech, he denounces Prohibition as "a smuggler and a fraud," and when the pertinacious lad clings desperately to his daddy, the unfaithful father raises his hand to heaven and says: "Oh! if I could alienate this Prohibition child of mine!" (Tremendous applause.)

I would ask Colonel Mills, if before Kansas was born, Prohibition was not a living issue in Texas, in 1854-55? And I would ask him if he was honest then, when he carried this "piratical flag at the masthead of his corsair?" And if he was honest then, as I believe, how dare he now denounce as hypocrites, men who occupy his old position? And if not honest then, how do we know he is not now flying another piratical flag at the masthead?

There is one flesh-mark of identification on that repudiated and dishinherited child, which Col. Mills can never obliterate. In 1855, that boy shouted: "Hurrah for Prohibition and Liberty!" The father's speech now betrays him. He has the same yell with only a change of two syllables. His slogan now is: "Hurrah for anti-Prohibition and Liberty!"

I will ask him again if in 1855 he honestly greeted the Prohibition minister of Christ as a servant of God, how dare he now denounce the ministry of Texas as "putting on the livery of heaven to serve the devil in"? Any traffic in the world that can so metamorphose such a man, is a bad business.

10. The final count in the indictment against the liquor traffic is that it has caused its advocates to re-open the vault of Thomas Jefferson and with felonious and burglarious hands take up the hallowed dust of the sage of Monticello, and scatter these sacred relics around the altar of that alcoholic despotism which the living Jefferson held in abhorrence. Never in any controversy has a great man been so misrepresented.

VIII

GOVERNOR ROSS ANSWERED

(An Open Letter Interrogating the Chief Executive.)

—oOo—

*Facts Concerning Maine, Iowa, Rhode
Island and Kansas — The Internal Revenue
License Argument Exploded
and Prohibition Vindicated.*

To Hon. L. S. Ross, Governor of Texas: —

If one may be allowed, without speaking evil of dignities, or bringing reproach upon the ruler of the people, to review your open letter to Mr. Gibbs, it would seem appropriate to do so now. While the individuality of the governor is never lost in official position, yet the official position makes you the governor of Prohibitionists, as well as of anti-Prohibitionists. What a private man speaks carries only the weight of its intrinsic worth. But what a high official utters carries all the weight borrowed from the dignity and sanctity of the office.

Because of your official relation to all the people, and because your private views on the pending amendment were already known to all men, some of your friends have thought it unseemly for you to throw the weight of your official position against this amendment which the publication of your letter most certainly does. Its influence upon the public mind will not stop at its intrinsic, individual worth, but will be more mighty as coming from the governor of Texas than from L. S. Ross. In precisely this direction the opponents of the amendment are using it for all the word "governor" is worth.

In these days of civil service reform, the idea gains ground among the people that it is not wise to use official position, the heritage of all the people, to carry measures that are favored by only a part of the people. This idea is stronger where the office is higher. Moreover the odds against the Prohibitionists were already appalling — not indeed as to unbiased popular judgment, but in the awful power of the liquor-traffic — its terrible organization and its unlimited control of money. It is reported that even ex-Governor Roberts thought it not wise, on account of his relation to the State University, to use that official position against the amendment.

But while thousands of your friends grieve that you have thought it necessary to write this letter, we will let that pass. You have written it, and what you have written you have written. You have lent to the whisky interests all the power of the gubernatorial name. It has made you solid with them. Your letter will be used as their chief campaign document. They will trade largely upon the governor's name.

And now that it is done, what remains to us? If we reply to it ever so respectfully it will be alleged that we are trying to damage your administration and hedge against you for a second term. No matter how carefully your letter is reviewed, it will amount to the same. The cry will be raised that we are trying to kill off Ross, seizing thereby upon another catch-penny phrase, to mislead the people. It may be that you have some enemies. It is hoped they will be silent as to your course.

But this letter is from your friend. One who has been such for long years. One who labored hard both for your nomination and election, and rejoiced in the privilege of voting for you. But since you have elected to enter this controversy it is held that your utterances become as much the legitimate subject of criticism as any other man's. Because it is not right to speak of dignitaries, to bring any railing accusation against them or to reproach the ruler of the people, this reply will, at present, ignore the governor and consider your campaign document, circulated by the liquor men.

As such a document, considered as an impersonal and anonymous communication, you will excuse me for saying that it would not attain much circulation. I mean to say that if it had been picked up in the road, undated and unsigned, but little money would have been wasted in its circulation. Placed side by side in this respect with Herrick Johnson's reply to Howard Crosby, in which the right ground, object and motive of prohibition are exhibited, your document would suffer much by the juxtaposition.

That paper of Johnson's undated and unsigned, might have been wafted to Texas shores by random winds or waves, and left discolored on a lonely beach, but the first man that read it, whether untutored or cultured, would have said: "This must not perish; it must be published; the people must read it; it will live; it cannot die!" But had yours so come, it is questionable whether its intrinsic merit would have saved it from a lasting silence on the lonely shore. There, with the other debris, washed up by restless waves, it would have perished, a valueless waif along with the pulpy jelly-fish around it.

But to the analysis: You plead the pleasure of official duty as an excuse for not taking an active part in the popular discussion. But. you see no impropriety in using your pen. The people will hardly recognize your distinctions. Whatever impropriety attaches to one attaches also to this and enters fully and squarely into the discussion of the whole matter. Your right to enter this field is fully conceded by this scribe. Some people may, indeed, question the propriety of it, but as tastes differ, we let that pass. Omitting any present reference to your preliminary observations, your objections to the amendment, when boiled down, are substanially these:

1. For fifty years Texas has prospered without this amendment, therefore it is unwise to adopt it.

2. There are shades of evil in the picture of the fifty years retrospect cast by the abuses of the liquor traffic, but there are only such evils and imperfections as cling to all the works of man, therefore, they are remediless by legislation. What is crooked cannot be made straight.

3. The laws, as they exist, are as competent to deal with these abuses as with other abuses.

4. These liquor evils are not sufficient to make a "pretext for innovations against Democratic policy."

5. Anti-prohibition Texas is ahead in material and moral development of prohibition states, and freer from pauperism and crime.

6. Internal revenue reports show that in Maine, Kansas and Iowa that liquor is still made and sold and the people of these states are robbed of legitimate revenue. Therefore it is unwise for Texas to rob itself of a million of revenue in order to promote the clandestine traffic.

7. Without this revenue we cannot keep the government and the schools running, except by largely increased taxation, which the people cannot bear.

8. You deny that the suppression of the traffic will appreciably reduce crime or the expenses for prosecuting crime.

9. You then make an appeal to the Holy Scriptures to substantiate your position.

10. Finally, you refer to the dismemberment of the Democratic party as political parricide which ought to be considered as Solon's law, an impossible crime, and only on this account unaccompanied with a condign penalty.

Such, fairly stated, and more strongly stated than in your paper, is your decalogue. Some men will wonder why you did not make the Holy Scriptures your climax. Why, as it succeeded in the ascending graduation of importance the preceding eight reasons, it was in turn succeeded and overshadowed by that higher and more sacred reason, the preservation of the Democratic party. You seem willing to concede the possibility of mutilating, dismembering and disobeying that Holy book, and hence, the wisdom of penalties for such violations of mere divine law, but to mutilate or dismember the Democratic party is in your sight a crime so inconceivable that an adequate punishment could not be named.

I say, some will wonder at your collocation, while others, in their stupidity, will wonder, why by your recommendation and approval you made this awful crime possible. If, as you allege, "the legislature submitted this question to a fair vote of the people in the fairest mode in which it could be done, that is, as an isolated issue unincumbered with other questions that might be a fair expression of the popular will upon it," then why do you now, you the governor who recommended and approved the measure, now writing and dating from the Executive office, complicate the issue and incumber it with other questions?

Why do you seek to thwart the legislative will, which refused to connect this with the general elections that it might be isolated from party politics? I say why do you now, against the published protest of seventy-six Democratic members of the legislature, seek to make this a party question and talk about Solon and his impossible crimes and suggest in connection with this "isolated and unincumbered issue," the political parricide of dismembering the Democratic party? It is questionable whether any just man in all T e x a s expected you to do such a thing.

And how could you write that sentence immediately after urging the people to calm deliberation at this hour, when the tide of feeling is running so high that its roar may drown for the time the great voice of reason?

Do you suppose that when you, in such a connection, talk "about pretext for innovation against

Democratic policy" and when you say "the dismemberment of the Democratic party ought to be treated as political parricide," that you have helped to allay "the tide of feeling" which you deprecate, or that you thereby hush "the roar that drowns the great voice of reason," or that you have aided to secure "calm deliberation," or that you have, with the legislature, left this issue, "isolated and unincumbered"?

Upon you, the governor of all Texas, the chief magistrate of Prohibitionists as well as of liquor dealers and their defenders, I respectfully press the inquiry: Have you helped to "a fair vote of the people" — have you assisted in securing "a fair expression of the popular will"?

When you see and know by the expressions in the papers that thousands upon thousands of Democrats desire to vote for this amendment as an "isolated and unincumbered question," but who do not desire to injure the Democratic party, you now, their governor and standard-bearer, come out before the world, and, upon just construction, intimate that for a Democrat to be a Prohibitionist is like murdering one's own father in that the adoption of this amendment will murder the Democratic party. In doing this you defeat the only thing under heaven the people asked for, that is, an "isolated and unincumbered issue."

They showed clearly by their votes, tens of thousands of Prohibitionists who voted for you against Dohoney, where they stood as Democrats, and that they did not seek to dismember the party. Having thus, in an unequivocal manner made plain their fealty to democracy, they then say, "Now let us vote on prohibition in a non-partisan election as a side issue."

You recommended that this be done. The legislature did this very thing as their published protest shows, but now, just on the eve of the anti-prohibition convention, when they, driven by the threats of the liquor dealers, are trying to muster up courage enough to make it a party question, you send out your pronunciamento giving to their deliberate conspiracy all the sanction of the gubernatorial name. By doing this you have made this much at least sure, that whenever hereafter in all the future you mix with fair-minded men, the finger of retribution will point to a withered flower in your chaplet of glory, while the voice of your royal justice will say, in the words of Bruce at Bannockburn: "Randolph, thy wreath hath lost a rose."

Every broken-hearted woman, widowed and penniless by the liquor traffic, will mark that withered flower on your brow and find in it a fit emblem of her own faded hopes and blasted joys. Every orphan made such by the traffic will lament as he looks hopelessly on the wreath adorning the head of his governor, the absence of that rose. Every real parricide — who maddened by whisky, murdered his own father on earth and blasphemed the name of his father in Heaven, when stung to never-dying death by the scorpions of remorse, will wonder with unspeakable wonder how it could be classed as parricide for a Democrat to vote against the whisky that makes parricides.

But I would ask you yet another question. Are you right sure that the course you have adopted is the very best one to guard against the dismemberment of the Democratic party? Will it add to the purity and numerical strength of that party for it to become a fixed principle of Democratic discipline that any one of its members is to be treated as a political parricide who favors the abolition of the whisky traffic?

I will venture another question: If the partisan issue which your words suggest and encourage is made in this canvass, is not that taking back with the gubernatorial left hand what the legislature granted with the right hand? And if prohibition is defeated by such tactics, will that settle the question to the satisfaction of the people?

Moreover, if you could beat us fairly and honorably before the people on a non-partisan issue, wouldn't that come nearer settling it than the way you suggest? Wouldn't it increase all good men's love for the Democratic party? Would it be likely to cost the Democratic party in the future one single vote? Wouldn't it be unanswerable and effectually stop future gains from Democratic ranks?

Again, haven't you practically conceded by your suggestion the invincible strength and immortality of the prohibition idea, when in addition to hundreds of thousands of dollars from the liquor men outside of Texas, in addition to Dr. Arch Cochran, and your reliance upon the Republican colored and the Bohemian vote, you yet think it necessary to array against prohibition the name of a party whose majority in Texas is 125,000?

It must be a strong principle that, without money, naked-handed, requires such a combination to defeat it. If prohibition is wrong, prove it. Why seek rather to prove it is anti-Democratic? Is it fairly courteous on your part to designate this movement as "a pretext for innovation on Democratic policy"?

Allow me to respectfully ask if there is any one word in all the official utterances of the Prohibition General Committee that by any just construction can warrant such an allegation. Have they, by one hair's breadth, swerved from their original declaration, that "we make this canvass as citizens of Texas, without reference to partisan politics or distinctions of race and religion"? Have they, in any one particular, gone outside of what you, yourself, say was the legislative intent in submitting this question "to a fair vote of the people, in the fairest mode in which it could be done, that is, as an isolated issue unencumbered with other questions?" Have they not even at the cost of friends and help, utterly left all moral and religious organizations to their own methods of work rigidly withholding any organic union with this committee? By what process of reasoning then can you justify your advice to the anti-prohibition convention?

Having thus noticed your last and most important reason for aligning yourself against prohibition, let us examine the next in value. You say: "After looking through the sacred book from Genesis to the end, I find an exhortation to every virtue and a rebuke for every sin, but I nowhere find the condemnation of the making or drinking of wine." This statement with amplification has appeared for many years in the campaign tracts issued by the distillers of sour mash whisky. Their tracts containing it are flooding Texas now. They always shelter the saloons and distillers behind Bible grape juice, as you do now.

To reply to this objection you well know would subject the Prohibition committee to the charge and prejudice of making a religious crusade. Any use of the Bible on their part in this discussion would be met with the objection that the sacred Scriptures are neither the constitution nor statute book of secular governments. That such a supposition implies a union of church and state, so justly obnoxious to every American citizen.

I would again respectfully propound to you other questions. Suppose it is proven that the Bible justifies State prohibition; will that be considered a settlement of this controversy? Only let that appear authoritatively, and no warhorse ever rushed more gladly to battle than prohibitionists would rejoice to accept the issue.

Reflect for a moment, and ask why the 4,000 preachers of Texas, who have made that book their life study, favor prohibition with such a remarkable approach to unanimity? There are doubtless exceptions, and honorable ones, but they are exceptions, so few in number, as to show more clearly by contrast the colossal outlines of the overwhelming majority.

Suppose the lawyers of Texas approached as nearly to unanimity in regard to certain legal propositions, would it not be accounted presumptuous in a man not a lawyer to affirm that they were all wrong in their interpretations of their own textbooks? And without going into the argument, is it not a fair presumption against your position, that preachers so nearly unanimously, and the Christians as a rule, have reached a different conclusion from your own?

Again from what part of this amendment do you find warrant for speaking of "drinking of wine"? Or where do you find in it a suggestion about "changing your moral convictions by force"? And by what conjuration do you find in it the "fires of inquisition"? And if you do find in it the "fires of inquisition" or the burning of "Massachusetts witches" ... if you do find them there, how could you reconcile it to your conscience to recommend the submitting of such an awful measure to a vote of the people? Are the gentlemen managing the prohibition campaign — many of them your fellow townsmen and your equals in both manhood and Democracy— are these gentlemen witch burners and inquisitors? Take the roll of their central committee and compare it with yours; take their club rolls and compare them with yours, and wherein on any point of respectability or Democracy, do they suffer by the comparison?

And what, allow me to ask, is the real value of your generalities about the fifty years prosperity of Texas, without prohibition? How much is such an argument worth? If it proves anything, it would prove that you ought not now to be governor, since Texas had gotten along so well with out you for fifty years. It would be equally forceful against all new measures. It would crystallize civilization and petrify progress and stop the mov-

ing hand upon the dial plate of time. You certainly
got this conceit from Washington Irving's Rip Van
Winkle.

And when you talk about the shades of evil
cast by the liquor traffic over your rose-colored
retrospect of fifty years, you certainly put it mild-
ly, considering the number and blackness of the
shadows.

But when you claim that present laws are
competent to deal with these abuses, you array
yourself against the most widely known and best
attested facts of history. There is not a farce en-
acted to-day on the boards of theatrical comedy, so
farcial as the failure of these laws. If there were
no tragedy mixed with it, we might laugh at the
farce and let it pass.

When you claim that anti-prohibition Texas is
ahead, in material and moral development, of prohibition states, your comparison is invidious, your
data unreliable and your logic faulty. Why compare
in material growth, a young, rising, western state
like Texas with an old, and cold and sterile state
like Maine? Have you never heard that, "Westward
the march of Empire takes its way"? Have you
forgotten Horace Greeley's advice to the young man?
And then why compare one state to another, instead
of comparing the same state before and after prohibition?

And then are you sure that the reports of crime
in Maine and Texas, or in Alabama and Maine, are
equally full and fair? May it not be that Maine, in
the reports to which you refer, tabulates more classes of offenses than the southern states to which you
and Col. Horace Chilton refer? I would suggest
that before you base any more arguments upon these
comparative statistics that you ascertain whether the
Maine-statistics cover wider ground and larger range
of offenses than the ones compared with it.

Suppose that one state reports only felonies and
the other all the cases before justice courts — or

suppose one reports all "drunks" and the other only the "ragamuffin" cases — or suppose one has a better system of statistics than the other and works it better, what then becomes of your argument based upon the invidious comparison? Had you not better look a little deeper into this matter, and go a little behind the statistical curtains?

My dear general, allow me to make a comparison. Suppose we compare your letter to Mr. Gibbs with your message to the legislature. The one is acknowledged by all men to be a masterly document of statecraft, surprisingly strong and wise. The other, I mean the Gibbs' letter, will generally be reckoned by the same judges, as the veriest twaddle of a demagogue. It is light as gossamer and as free from the cream of argument as the blue, skimmed milk from a poor cow.

Occupying the position you do with the opportunities of information at hand, your statement about the workings of Texas laws would be entitled to credit more than the immature utterances of a stranger. This being true, has it not occurred to you that the carefully revised statements of the governors of prohibition states, as embodied in their messages, and as disclosing the workings of law in their states, furnish more reliable and assuring data than any unripe statement to the contrary on your part?

Do you know more about Maine than its governor? Are you better posted in Kansas affairs than Governor Martin? Is it a fair presumption that Governor Larrabee, of Iowa, would gain wisdom in the criminal statistics of his own state, by paying a visit to the Executive Mansion in Austin?

Are you in a position to know more of crime and its costs in Rhode Island than its chief of police? The kind of talk that you now talk is like the talk of Gov. Martin of Kansas, before prohibition was tried. In his biennial message of this year,

1887, he talks quite differently. In exchanging gubernatorial civilities would it not be well for you to exchange messages?

If I did not think you would regard it as impertinent I would be pleased to call attention to some things the public officials of prohibition states have placed on record — the testimony of governors, judges, attorneys, police chiefs, merchants and mechanics. If human testimony can establish any earthly proposition, this evidence will conclusively show your statement to be a groundless assumption.

Your reference to the revenue reports and the conclusions arrived at from them indicate, if you will excuse the statement, how little you have really studied the subject and how ill-prepared you are to speak dogmatically concerning it. It is nothing to the United States how many people pay for a revenue license. It is good for one year when paid for and is counted one, and so goes into the reports. The United States never stops to inquire what becomes of the man until the next pay-day. But allow me to show your excellency that the number of these licenses issued in Prohibition states prove nothing as to the amount of liquor sold, though they may exceed the number issued before prohibition laws became operative. Some of them are as follows:

1. In one town in Kansas where twenty-one permits were granted and paid for and included in the United States revenue reports, nineteen of these liquor sellers were in jail for violating the law, the others skipped the country, and the town did not have an open grog-shop during the year, though the United States revenue reports would indicate twenty-one.

2. In the city of Topeka at one place of business, seven men in rapid succession paid each for such a permit, each permit being reported in the United States Revenue reports, though in seven weeks' time all these sellers were in turn suppressed by the vindicators of a violated law. Had there been no

prohibition law there would have been only one license for this one place of business. But under prohibitory law the licenses increased sevenfold and yet there was no saloon and no one of the seven operated but for a few days. Now here are seven licenses under prohibition against one before prohibition, and the one before prohibition sold a thousandfold more liquor than the seven after prohibition because the seven were one by one suppressed in a few days.

3. It is a fact, as well established as that you are governor, that when the man paying the license does escape suppression, he yet, on account of the clandestine methods necessary to evade law, sells not a tithe of the amount that he did when he ran an open saloon.

So you may see that the United States revenue reports prove nothing as to amounts sold. They only prove that the federal government did not bother him, and hinder his sales. The state's case against him is another matter. How simple then your question: "Will any candid and fair man contend that this liquor was not consumed by the people?"

What liquor, my dear governor, what liquor? The United States which received that money did not guarantee a market. Did not guarantee against state suppression. It merely guaranteed against interference by the federal government. If you'll have a talk with old Anheuser Busch and the president of the Liquor Dealers National Protective Association, they will explain this little matter to you. They know what it means. That's why they are sending hundreds of thousands of dollars into Texas to defeat this amendment. To them those United States revenue statistics, that you find so toothsome, sound as hollow as an empty whisky barrel or dry beer keg.

Suppose just for a change, you read up a little on their annual meeting, listen to their doleful lamentation, and then offer them these revenue reports for food, and they will tell you they are as empty of meat to them as a blasted nut. And don't you see, besides, that in reporting Iowa at $2,500,000 up to June 30, 1886, you include the licenses issued before the law had practical operations? In that $2,500,000 is the money paid by Sioux City Saloon men — I mean the men who are charged with murdering Haddock, but though Uncle Sam has the revenue all right — where are the saloons to-day? And in the $208,000 from Kansas is the amount paid by the 276 saloons from Leavenworth and the saloons which lined both sides of the main street of Topeka — five miles long. But where are the saloons to-day and where are the saloon men?

So when you ask, "What have the states which adopted the prohibitory laws secured as a compensation for long agitation of this question with all of its paralyzing divisions and discussions?" I have a notion to tell you. Your questions will be forwarded to the governors of these states, but while waiting for a fresh answer to your rather ill-advised criticisms of their internal affairs, you must be content with the following which is nearly fresh. Gov. Martin of Kansas, in his biennial message 1887, this year, mark you, thus answers your question:

"A great reform has certainly been accomplished in Kansas. Intemperance is steadily and surely decreasing. In thousands of homes where want and wretchedness and suffering were once familiar guests, plenty, happiness and contentment now abide. Thousands of wives and children are better clothed and fed than they were when the saloons absorbed all the earnings of the husbands and fathers. The marvelous material growth of the state during the past six years has been accompanied by an equally marvelous moral progress, and it can be fairly and truthfully asserted that in no portion of the civilized world can a million and a half of people be found who are more temperate than the people of Kansas.

"There is not an observing man in the state who does not know that a great reform has been accomplished in Kansas by prohibition. There is not a truthful man in the state who will not frankly acknowledge this fact no matter what his opinions touching the policy of prohibition may have been.

"The public sentiment of Kansas is overwhelmingly against the liquor traffic. Thousands of men who a few years ago opposed prohibition, or doubted whether it was the best method of dealing with the liquor traffic have seen and frankly acknowledge its beneficial results and its practical success. The temptations with which the open saloon allured the youth of the land to disgrace and destruction; the appetite for liquor bred and matured within its walls by the treating custom; the vice, crime, poverty, suffering and sorrow of which it is always the fruitful source, all these evil results of the open saloon have been abolished in nearly every city and town in Kansas."

Here is a message from Iowa:

Des Moines, Iowa, April 21, —

Governor Larrabee has written a letter in reply to an inquiry from the secretary of the central committee of the prohibitory campaign of Texas in regard to the workings of prohibition in Iowa. The governor says, "In eighty out of the ninety-nine counties of the state prohibition is enforced, and in the remaining nineteen counties it is partly enforced; no property has been depreciated by its enforcement, as saloons make room for better and more legitimate business; the enforcement of the law has had no noticeable effect upon the population beyond causing the removal from the state of some incurable dispensers and perhaps some incurable consumers." The effects of prohibition upon the general welfare and habits of the people, he says, are decidedly wholesome. The prohibition sentiment is on the increase, and there is no doubt that prohibition is an established power in Iowa.

We also append the following telegram, from the commissioner of labor statistics:

"Des Moines, Iowa, March 23, —

Governor and attorney-general both say prohibition has constantly improved the moral, social and financial condition of Iowa, and is successfully enforced in eighty-five of the ninety-nine counties, also growing rapidly in the remainder.

E. R. Huchins."

On February 3, 1887, Gov. Larrabee also said: "I find in the cities and counties where the prohibitory law is well enforced, crime and police expenses fall off wonderfully. Not a saloon is open in this, the largest city in the state. The sheriff of this county told me a few days since that he had spoiled his business by enforcing the law. He also stated that he was glad of it. Several of the judges have recently told me that there was a marked falling off in criminal business in their courts in consequence of the enforcement of the law. There are several judicial districts without a single open saloon. If our courts and sheriffs and constables would do their duty properly the saloons would soon be completely driven out."

And here is one from Rhode Island. Hon. George P. Wetmore, governor of Rhode Island, in his annual address, 1887, said:

"All things considered I think it may be said that as good results have been obtained from its enforcement as could have reasonably been anticipated, and as evidence of this I may cite the official records of the police departments of the cities of Providence and Newport, whose statements, which I assume to be correct, indicate a large reduction of drunkenness and of that class of disorder and misery which intoxicants provoke and stimulate."

In the same connection I append two telegrams sent out during the recent Michigan campaign:

"Providence, R. I., March 23, —

Increase of arrests for drunkenness and revelry in Providence last six months license, over 18 per cent. Decrease in first six months prohibition, over 42 per cent. Common drunkenness in same time decreased in Newport, 100 per cent; Pawtucket, 50 per cent; last two months, 75 per cent. Official figures.

H. W. Conant."

"Providence, R. I., March 24, —

The statistics from the city of Providence, the largest city in the state, show an increase of drunkenness during the last six months of the license law, of 183 per cent. While during the first six months of prohibition, as compared with the corresponding period under license, drunkenness decreased more than 42 per cent. The commitments to the state workhouse, whose inmates are largely victims of the intemperate use of intoxicating liquors, for the first six months of prohibition as compared with the corresponding period under license, show a falling off of more than one-half, and resulting in the large saving to the state of more than $1,800,000 per annum in the item of board alone.

"The 'Growler' or tin kettle trade has almost entirely disappeared from the streets, and children are not now seen frequenting liquor saloons for supplies of liquor as before prohibition went into effect. Many families that never saw a penny of the weekly earnings of its head, now receive the full benefit of its labors. The legislature now in session has indefinitely postponed, by an almost unanimous vote, a propositioin to submit the repeal of the prohibition amendment to the people, and will at this session make the prohibition law more effective.

C. R. Brayton,

Chief of State Police."

And here is one from the governor of Maine:

"Augusta, Maine, March 23, —

The finances of the state never more prosperous. Drink habit is fatal to prosperity in any community. Prohibition promotes morality everywhere. Nearly all crimes can be placed to rum either directly or indirectly. The law is well enforced in the country towns. In some of the cities it is not quite so effective. It is hoped that the new law will aid the enforcement there.

Joseph R. Bodwell."

And now if your excellency will bear with me a little while I will submit a document that is marvelously like your letter and like the platform adopted by the Anti-Prohibitionists at Dallas. It is the testimony of Gov. Martin, of Kansas, six years ago, before he tried prohibition. It reads thus:

"I opposed the adoption of the amendment for three principal reasons:
"First, because it was an unwise and unlawful infringement upon individual liberty, and an assumption of power beyond the legitimate functions of civil government.
"Second, because its honest enforcement would be impossible and will utterly fail in accomplishing

the object of its friends, and in the end produce evils more perilous than all the drunkards and grog-shops in the land.

"Now, has the law been enforced? No! Will it be enforced? No! Why? Because it does violence to public judgment; is injudicious, violent, extreme, fanatical, an unlawful and unjust exercise of power, the result of ignorance, stupidity, and fanaticism.

"Third, another objection to the amendment and law is, it develops and brings to the front a class of hypocrites, spies, detectives, liars and informers — the most loathsome and offensive class of vermin that can possibly affect the body politic. This is the class of men fostered, encouraged and sustained by the law last winter — a class more dangerous to the peace, good order and safety of society than common murderers or highway robbers.

"Men from all parts of the globe, with known habits, customs and peculiarities have been by the direct agency of the state, invited and urged to come to our state, with the assurance that these habits would be recognized and protected — that they could at least enjoy the same degree of personal freedom they did in Europe. That the amendment will keep emigrants from our state, I think perfectly plain."

I ask you to note, first, that "spy" part of it and compare it with the spy-plank of the Dallas platform. And will you note this fact? Six years ago Martin stood where you do now. May we not reasonably hope that, this amendment being adopted in August, the last message of your second term will show you standing where Martin does now? It is true this does not allow six years for your conversion, but what Texan will admit that it will take more than three years for our "Little Calvary man" to ride over as much ground as a slow-poking Kansas man can cover in six years? And then, my dear general, if not sooner, you will forgive these candid, but kind strictures from your old friend, who remains as ever, yours for prohibition,

B. H. Carroll,

Chairman Prohibition Executive Committee.

P. S. Out of kindness I did not inflict upon you a certificate from J. G. Blaine as I thought that Dr. Arch Cochran was about all you could reasonably stand for a while.

B. H. C.

IX

PARAPHRASE OF THE DALLAS PLATFORM

(At the conclusion of his Austin speech.)

"We shall never see its like again!" Yes, fellow citizens, when in after ages the antiquarian shall brush the mouldering dust from its crumbling tombstone in order to decipher on the inscription the name of its author, he may well strike a funeral attitude and thus apostrophize this immortal document:

"It has fallen! We may now pause before that splendid prodigy, which towered among us like some ancient ruin, whose power crucified the politicians its magnificence attracted.

"Grand, gloomy and peculiar, it sat upon the throne of platforms a sceptered nondescript, wrapped in the solitude of its own originality; a platform Democratic, Republican and Independent; a platform blue as the skies and black as Africa; a platform that distances competition, uniqueness and pliable to every touch of interest, marked the outlines of this extraordinary document, the most extraordinary, perhaps that in the annals of this world ever rose or reigned or fell.

"Flung in the arena in the midst of an agitation that quickened every energy of a convention which acknowledged no party obligations, it commenced its course a stranger by suggestion, an orphan by birth, and may be styled a scholar by charity.

"With no authority but its word and no fortune but Anheuser's, it rushed into the list where truth, honor and patriotism had arrayed themselves, but the people fled from its embrace as from the glance of a pestilence.

"It knew no motive but interest; acknowledged no criterion but success; it worshipped no God but

— 101 —

Mammon and Bacchus, and with an eternal devotion it knelt at the shrine of idolatry.

"Subsidiary to this there was no creed that it did not profess; there was no adoption it did not promulgate. In the name of mustang grapes it upheld the distillery; for the sake of mash it bowed before a blackberry bush; the orphan of St. Louis, it claimed to be the adopted child of Texas; and with a parricidal ingratitude on the shame of both Democrats and Republicans, it reared the throne of alcoholic despotism.

"A professed Democrat, it pilloried Coke; a pretended Republican, it repelled Cuney, and in the name of Jefferson it grasped without remorse and shook without shame the Hamiltonian hand of Arch Cochran. The whole state shook with laughter at the mendacity of its designs and the miracle of their execution. Skepticism bowed to the prodigies of its allegations, nor was there aught too incredible for belief or too fanciful for expectation when the world saw a subaltern of Corsicana waving the democratic flag at the head of the shouting column of its ancient enemies.

"All the platforms of antiquity became commonplace beside this. It matters little whether they were written in the field or in the drawing room, at the head of a mob or on a levee. Amid all comparisons this platform stands unique and unapproachable, whether you consider it as wearing a Democratic bonnet or a Republican crown, ostracising Coke, Reagan, Maxey, and Culberson, or espousing Melvin Wade. In this wonderful combination its affectations of liberty and temperance must not be omitted.

"The jailer and subsidizer of the press, the proscriber of opinions, the persecutor of free speech and the boycotter of trade, the incubator of rotten eggs, it talks of 'personal liberty.' The same watchword is in the mouth of the anarchist, and a similar platform sheltered the assassins of Haddock, and in the name of temperance it seeks to fasten the saloons forever upon a free people.

"Such a medley of contradictions and at the same time a lack of consistency were never before united in the same platform. A Democrat, a Republican and an Independent; a know-nothing, a Catholic, and a patron of the synagogue; a Christian, an infidel, and through all its checkered contrarieties, the same mysterious, incomprehensible document, a platform without a model and without a shadow."

X

AN INTERROGATION OF THE ANTIS CONCERNING MR. JEFFERSON, THE DALLAS PLATFORM AND SUMPTUARY LAWS.

To the Editor of the Advance:

Mr. Gibbs and others, as a committee appointed by Judge Clark and others, in their private letters to Coke, Reagan, Maxey, Culberson and others, say: "The object of the Dallas convention is to set forth clearly and unequivocally the time-honored and cardinal principles of the Democratic party from Jefferson down to the present time, viz: opposition to all forms of sumptuary legislation."

The Austin call, issued by the same gentlemen, numbers, as the first-class invited to the Dallas convention, the following: "All followers of Thomas Jefferson and who believe with him that government is best which governs least."

While the Dallas platform adopted by this convention discreetly omits the name of Jefferson (possibly out of deference to Dr. Cochran and Melvin Wade) its second plank says: "We oppose this amendment because it is sumptuary, etc."

Now concerning these three publications we submit the following inquiries:

1. Will any member of the Driskill convention, or any member of their "Letter committee," or any member of the Dallas platform committee, please inform us when and where any Democratic national convention, prior to 1876, incorporated in its platform an anti-sumptuary plank?

2. Will they also interpret for us, since they class Mr. Jefferson as anti-sumptuary, the following declarations of Mr. Jefferson?

"Paris, July 28, 1787.

To Mr. Shipworth:

Dear Sir: — . . . All my letters are filled with details of our extravagance. From these accounts I look back to the time of the war as a time of happiness and enjoyment, when amidst the privations of many things not essential to happiness we could not run in debt, because nobody would trust us; when we practised by necessity the maxim of buying nothing but what we had the money in our pockets for; a maxim which of all others, lays the broadest foundations for our happiness. I see no remedy to our evils, but an open course of law. Harsh as it may seem, it would relieve the patients who dread it, by stopping the course of their extravagance, before it renders their affairs entirely desperate.

Thomas Jefferson."

For other expressions in the same direction see letter to A. Donal, July 1787, in which he says:

"I know of no remedy against indolence and extravagance but a free course of justice. I l o o k forward to the abolition of all credit."

See also his letter to William Hay, August 4, 1787, in which he says: "What is to extricate us I know not, whether law or loss of credit."

3. Will they also inform us why the general index to Mr. Jefferson's works, tabulating a vast variety of topics discussed by himself, of law, philosophy, agriculture, commerce and hundreds of other things, makes no reference by name to sumptuary laws?

4. Will they also inform us how it is that Roman sumptuary laws, and the English sumptuary

laws, in force from Edward III to Henry VIII, in neither case prohibited the liquor traffic?

5. Will they kindly furnish us with the name of any competent legal authority of Jefferson's time that classified prohibition of the liquor traffic as sumptuary?

6. If it was so classified, did not Mr. Jefferson recommend the enactment of sumptuary legislation, when in his special message of Jan. 28, 1802 he advised Congress to prohibit the liquor traffic with the Indians because of its "baneful effects on their morals, their health and existence"?

Please understand that while favoring a restriction of the liquor traffic to useful purposes, such as medicinal, scientific, sacramental and mechanical, prohibition Democrats are themselves opposed to sumptuary laws. What we desire for modern Jeffersonians, who make a fetish of his name, is that when they appeal to Caesar, unto Caesar must they go.

7. Since their platform goes into spasms of alarm over the danger to the infant industry of grape culture for winemaking, why do they not cite Mr. Jefferson's great letter advising his countrymen to go into olive culture and let alone "the desperate gambling of grape culture" for wine making? (See letter to Wm. Drayton, written from Paris, July 30, 1787 — I wonder if Judge Clark's organ will ever publish this letter.)

8. Since this platform designates prohibition of the liquor traffic for beverage purposes as a "species of paternalism," to what species will they relegate Mr. Jefferson's document on lotteries and games of chance, in which he says, "cards, dice and billiards are entirely unproductive, doing good to none, injury to many, yet so easy, and so seducing in practice to men of a certain constitution of mind that they cannot resist the temptation, be the consequences what they may, that in this case, as in those of insanity, idiocy, infancy, etc., it is the duty of society

to take them under its protection even against
their own acts, and to restrain their right of choice
of these pursuits by suppressing them entirely."

I wonder if the "personal liberty" men of to-
day would call this "a species of paternalism." And
I further wonder if the anti-prohibition papers of
the state will publish these questions as a campaign
document.

9. Since their platform says that the proposed
amendment, which seeks only to restrict the traffic in intoxicating liquors to the four useful purposes named, will "take from the citizen his most
sacred and inalienable rights," will they please inform us from what item of Mr. Jefferson's bill of
rights do they draw the conclusion? Will it take
away "freedom of religion; or freedom of the press;
or create monopolies and standing armies; or sus-
pend the habeas corpus, or suppress the right to
trial by juries"? And if to make or sell intoxicating
liquors is the citizen's most sacred and inalienable
right, did Mr. Jefferson himself ever enjoy this right?
Did prohibition in Iowa take away from the alleged
murderers of Haddock the right of trial by jury?

10. Finally, if, as their platform alleges, the
adoption of this amendment will cause our "homes
to be searched and our property seized," how will it
be able to stand before the fourth amendment to
the constitution, inserted largely through Mr. Jefferson's instrumentality, and which reads:

"The right of the people to be secure in their
persons, houses, papers and effects, against unrea-
sonable searches and seizures, shall not be violated;
and no warrants shall issue but upon probable cause,
supported by oath or affirmation, and particularly
describing the place to be searched and the person
or thing to be seized"?

And if there be any seizures and searches in
accordance with this amendment, how is the law a
tyranny? And how does it invade the right of the
citizens? And if the amendment "purposes to change

our form of government from a free republic of sovereign and independent citizens," how can it stand before section 4, article 4, of the federal constitution which reads:

"The United States shall guarantee to every state in this union a republican form of government," etc? Anti-prohibition organs and orators, please answer.

XI

THOMAS JEFFERSON AND THE
PRESENT ISSUE

(Article by B. H. Carroll and Dr. Robinson.)

To the Editor of the Ādvance:

Continuing the subject introduced in your Sunday issue, we here insert a declaration of Mr. Jefferson concerning

OFFICE AND ARDENT SPIRITS:

"The habit of using ardent spirits by men in public office has occasioned more injury to the public service and more trouble to me than any other circumstance which has occurred in the internal concerns of the country during my administration, and were I to commence my administration again, with the knowledge which from experience I have acquired, the first question I would ask in regard to an application for office should be: Is he addicted to the use of ardent spirits?

Thomas Jefferson."

This statement is clipped from the Clarksville Standard, edited by the "Veteran of Texas Democracy," Chas. DeMorse. We have not yet had time to verify its accuracy from Mr. Jefferson's works but assume that it is correct.

In our first article we referred to Mr. Jefferson's letter to M. de Neuville in which, while calling whisky a "poison" and "a bane" he favors the encouragement of importation of light wines, by abating high duties. What he says, on this subject of importation, does not affect the pending amendment. But as it may be claimed that he was also an advocate of the home manufacture of wines, I here submit a pointed and pertinent extract from him on

GRAPE CULTURE IN THE UNITED STATES:

"Paris, July 30, 1787.

"To William Drayton:

"Sir: — . . . I was induced, in the course of my journey through the south of France, to pay very particular attention to the objects of their culture, because the resemblance of their climate to that of the southern states of the United Staes auhorizes us to presume we may adopt any of their articles of culture, which we would wish for. We should not wish for their wines, though they are good and abundant. The culture of the vine is not desirable in lands capable of producing anything else. It is a species of gambling, and of desperate gambling too, wherein, whether you make much or nothing, you are equally ruined.

"The middling crop alone is the saving point and that the seasons seldom hit. Accordingly, we see much wretchedness among this class of cultivators. Wine, too, is so cheap in these countries that a laborer with us, employed in the culture of any other article, may exchange it for wine, more and better than he could raise himself. It is a resource for a country, the whole of whose good soil is otherwise employed, and which has still some barren spots and surplus of population to employ on them. There the vine is good, because it is something in the place of nothing.

"It may become a resource to us at a still later period; when the increase of population shall increase our productions beyond the demand for them, both at home and abroad, instead of going on to make a useless surplus of them, we may employ our supernumerary hands on the vine. But that period has not yet arrived.

Thomas Jefferson."

Here is a rich production. As it is purely Jeffersonian, will the anti-prohibition organ publish it as a campaign document? And will it send marked copies to Messrs. Seth Sheppard, Barney Gibbs and Horace Chilton?

It may check the flow of tears so profusely falling from anti-prohibition cheeks over the danger which menaces "this dear infant, baby industry." They are bound to take this "grape prescription" which comes from their own doctor. But whether they "boil it or cool it" the dose will remain unpalatable.

It is suggested to all prohibition speakers and newspapers that they keep this Jeffersonian medicine, and whenever the antis become a little frantic shouting, "Grapes, Grapes, Grapes! Don't throttle the growing grape culture!" — then let the "prohib" according to the symptoms of the patient administer this Jeffersonian cure.

When Texas has no longer any good soil unemployed, when our population is as dense as Europe's, when our valuable productions exceed demands at home and abroad, and when our supernumerary laborers have nothing else to do, then it may be well to cultivate grapes as something is better than nothing. But even then it will be a species of desperate gambling, which whether you win or lose, will ruin you. However wry a face it may make for them let no anti repudiate Jefferson.

To vary matters for them we now change from "grape to solid shot." They have tried to use the party lash. They have tried to browbeat a verdict by partisan warfare. They have talked much of innovation and parricide, in connection with the dear old Democratic party! They have even employed

— 111 —

Dr. Arch Cochran and Melvin Wade to help them prove that prohibition is un-Jeffersonian and un-Democratic.

Under this hue and cry they have coerced some timid and unthinking ones to forswear their true convictions for the party's sake. As now all this has been done in the name of Jefferson and derived efficacy by that fetish, I here submit as an antidote what may be styled the natural right of each generation to change the constitution of the preceding. No law is binding longer than nineteen years.

LETTER TO JAMES MADISON

"Paris, Sept. 6, 1789.

". . . The question whether one generation of men has a right to bind another seems never to have been started, either on this, or our side of the water. Yet it is a question of such consequences, as not only to merit decision, but a place also among the fundamental principles of government. That no such obligation can be transmitted I think very capable of proof. If set out on this ground, which I suppose to be self-evident, that the earth belongs in use of such to the living; that the dead have neither powers nor rights over it.

". . . I say the earth belongs to each generation during its course, fully and in its own right. The second generation receives it clear of the debts and incumbrances of the first, the third of the second, and so on. For if the first could charge it with a debt, then the earth would belong to the dead, and not to the living generation. Then no generation can contract debts greater than may be paid during the course of its own existence.

". . . Neither the legislature nor the nation itself can validly contract more debt than may be paid within its own age.

". . . On similar ground it may be proved that

no society can make a perpetual constitution or a perpetual law. The earth belongs always to the living generation; they may manage it as they please during their usufruct. Every constitution, then, and every law naturally expires at the end of thirty-four years. If it be enforced longer it is an act of force and not of right."

Very soon after this letter to Mr. Madison, he wrote to Dr. Gem on the same subject, and at the close of the letter he makes this reflection:

"Half of those of twenty-one years and upward living at any one instant of time, will be dead in eighteen years and eight months, or say, nineteen years. Then the contracts, constitutions, and laws of every such society become void in nineteen years from their dates."

But these worshippers of a defunct past say: "Why amend the constitution? Why change the organic law? We have been doing well for fifty years. Why not let well enough alone?" We will let the sage of Monticello answer.

"Monticello, May 28, 1816.

"To John Taylor:

"Dear Sir: — ... If, then, the control of the people over the organs of their government be the measure of republicanism, and I confess I know no other measure, it must be agreed that our governments have much less republicanism than ought to have been expected; in other words, that the people have less regular control over their agents, than their rights and their interest require. And this I ascribe ... to speculators on government, whose fears of the people have been inspired by the populace of their own great cities, and were unjustly entertained against the independent, the happy, and therefore the orderly citizens of the United States.

"... The functionaries of public power rarely

strengthen in their dispositions to abridge it, and an unorganized call for a timely amendment is not likely to prevail against an organized opposition to it. We are always told that things are going on well. Why change them?

'Chi sta bene, non so mouve,' said the Italian: 'Let him who stands well, stand still.' This is true; and I verily believe they would go well with us under an absolute monarch, while our present character remains, of order, industry and love of peace, and restrained, as he (the monarch) would be, by the proper spirit of the people. But it is while it remains such, we should provide against the consequences of deterioration. . . . Governments are more or less republican, as they have more or less of the element of popular election and control in their composition; and believing as I do, that the mass of the citizens is the safest depository of their own rights, and especially, that the evils, following from the duperies of the people, are less injurious than those from the egoism of their agents, I am a friend of that composition of government which has in it the most of this ingredient.

Thomas Jefferson."

This is why we prefer to submit "this timely amendment" to the people themselves as safer "depositories of their own rights" than can be found in the "egoism of their agents," the legislature.

MR. JEFFERSON AND THE PARTY LASH

"Paris, March 13, 1789.

"To F. Hopkinson:

"Dear Sir — . . . You say that I have been dished up to you as an anti-Federalist, and ask me if it be just. My opinion was never worthy enough of notice to merit citing; but since you ask it, I will tell you. I am not a Federalist, because I never submitted the whole system of my opinions to the creed of any party of men whatever, in religion, in philosophy, in politics, or in anything else, where I was capable of thinking for myself. *Such an addiction is the last degradation of a free and moral agent. If I could not go to heaven without a party, I would not go there at all.* Therefore, I protest to you, I am not of the party of Federalists. But I am much farther from that of the anti-Federalists. . . . . These, my dear friend, are my sentiments, by which you will see I was right in saying, I am neither a Federalist nor an anti-Federalist; that I am of neither party, nor yet a trimmer between parties.

Thomas Jefferson."

And if, to-day the venerable shade of the sage of Monticello could be called up from the "vasty deep," he would say to Texas: "I have been dished up to you as being an anti-prohibitionist. If my opinion is worth citing, I would say that, while I am not an extreme prohibitionist, I am further from being an anti-prohibitionist."

From a careful survey of all his writings, we may justly reach the conclusion that his best living representative to-day, on this question, is Charles DeMorse, of the Clarksville Standard, the "veteran of Texas Democracy," who will vote for the pending amendment. We come now to consider

MR. JEFFERSON AND THE BILL OF RIGHTS.

Anti-prohibition orators, particularly C o l o n e l Mills, have exhausted declamation in telling how Mr. Jefferson, then in Paris, after reading the constitution of 1787, demanded the addition of a bill of rights. And so the Dallas platform introduced by Mr. Mills, as chairman, "opposes the pending amendment because it is a proposition to change our form of government, etc., and because it will take from the citizen his most sacred and inalienable right. Second, and that it was to secure this right, Mr. Jefferson called so loudly for a bill of rights."

To relieve Mr. Jefferson from this slander on his memory it is now proposed to let him speak for himself. He has been dead a long time. His works are out of print. They are found in but few libraries. The majority of those who roll his name under their tongue as a sweet morsel never read a line of his except the Declaration of Independence. This statement does not apply to Col. Mills. It would be better for him if it did. For then he could plead ignorance. We will now catechize the great American commoner: "Mr. Jefferson, when you demanded a bill of rights what did you mean? Were you thinking at all about saving the liquor traffic?" He answers promptly:

"What I meant by a bill of rights and what I regarded as defects in the federal constitution, is clearly set forth in my published letters to Madison, Carrington, Donald, Washington, Brown, Carmichael, Rutledge, Jay, Short, Hopkinson, Humphreys and others, and in my inaugural message."

Having examined carefully all these authorities, we now say to the people of Texas, that in them all there is not even a hint to the liquor traffic. His words are clear and express. In a number of those letters the very same words are used. What he says to one, he says to another. He employs no dubious generalities and equivocations. And as what he says to Madison is in every substantial particular, what he elsewhere says to others, we will only quote his

LETTER TO JAMES MADISON.

Paris, Dec. 20, 1787.

". . . . I will now tell you what I do not like.

First, the omission of a bill of rights, providing clearly and without the aid of sophism for freedom of religion, freedom of the press, protection against standing armies, restriction of monopolies, the eternal and unremitting force of the habeas corpus laws and trial by jury in all matters of fact, triable by the laws of the land, and not by the laws of nations."

From Paris, Dec. 21, 1787, he writes the same to Mr. E. Carrington, page 277. Again to A. Donald, page 291, from Paris, Feb. 6th, 1789. A second letter to James Madison, under date of July 31st, 1788, he writes from Paris, reiterating the same explanation of a bill of rights, page 343. To F. Hopkinson, page 438, he writes from Paris on March 13th, 1789, setting forth the same identical summary of rights without a single change. These pages refer to Vol. 2 of Randolph's Jefferson.

In his inaugural message he classes among the essential principles of our government "jealous care of the right of election by the people," and "absolute acquiesence in the decisions of the majority, the vital principles of republics, from which there is no appeal to force, the vital principle of and immediate parent of despotism."

Mr. Jefferson never dreamed of classing the sale and manufacture of whisky among the "most sacred and inalienable rights of the citizen." He himself never enjoyed such a right. He called whisky "a bane" and "a poison."

He didn't believe any man ought to hold office who was addicted to the use of ardent spirits. He recommended congress to prohibit the traffic to the Indians. And, for economic reasons, he advised his people to let alone "the desperate gambling of grape culture for wine."

MR. JEFFERSON AND THE SUPPRESSION OF NATURAL RIGHTS FOR THE PUBLIC GOOD.

In a petition to the Virginia legislature he thus

discusses "games of chance" (Washington's works of Jefferson, Vol. 9, pp. 501-502 and 505): "But there are some (games) which produce nothing, and endanger the well-being of the individuals engaged in them, or of others depending on them. Such are games of cards, dice, billiards, etc. Although the pursuit of them is a matter of natural right, yet, society, perceiving the irresistible bent of some of its members to pursue them and the ruin produced by them to the families depending on these individuals, considering it as a case of insanity, *quoad hoc*, steps in to protect the family and the party himself as in other cases of insanity, infancy, imbecility, etc. and suppresses the pursuit altogether, and the natural right of following it."

Again, "such games as cards, dice, etc., are entirely unproductive, doing good to none, injury to many, yet so easy and so seducing in practice to men of a certain constitution of mind, that they can not resist the temptation, be the consequences what they may; that in this case, as in those of insanity, idiocy, infancy, etc., it is the duty of society to take them under their protection, even against their own acts, and to restrain their right of choice of these pursuits, by suppressing them entirely."

In the same connection he brings out a principle of partnership intensely applicable to the licensing of the liquor traffic concerning what he regards as innocent lotteries; he says,

"This, then, is a declaration by the nation, that an act was not immoral, of which they were in the habitual use themselves as a part of the regular means of supporting the government. The tax on the vender of tickets was their share of the profits, and if their share was innocent, his could not be criminal."

This all makes good reading for our "personal liberty" friends. It may not be palatable but it is sound Jeffersonian doctrine, and they must not deny it or repudiate it. They must not go off on the line of the Dallas Herald's pictured Indian:

"Ingun big personal liberty man. Ingun must have whisky. Ingun get big drunk and beat squaw. Ingun go naked when he please, get drunk when he please, beat squaw when he please, big personal liberty man! Pale face big fool. Got too much law."

In the same direction we quote what Mr. Jefferson says is the paramount law, viz:

"To save the republic, the first and supreme law." Jefferson's memoirs, Vol. 1, p. 66-7. . . . "Honest error must be arrested, where its toleration leads to public ruin. As, for the safety of society, we cannot commit honest maniacs to Bedlam, so judges should be withdrawn from their bench, whose erroneous biases are leading us to dissolution. It may, indeed, injure them in fame or fortune, but it saves the republic, which is the first and supreme law."

But as some desire to worship antiquity, and they continually cry out, "The fathers, the fathers," and want us to have a cast-iron, inflexible, immutable constitution and make no provision for development and progress, and as the effort is being made in Jefferson's name, to petrify and crystallize civilization, we herewith submit another extract.

For discussing the prohibition of the liquor traffic, where the issue is confessedly non-partisan and where no office or political preferment is involved, preachers have been denounced and slandered by self-styled disciples of Jefferson. To offset these foul aspersions and misrepresentations we cite Mr. Jefferson again.

In his Memoirs, pp. 5 and 6, he thus describes a crisis, a political crisis, where the precahers' help was invoked, thus:

"We were under conviction of the necessity of arousing the people from the lethargy into which they had fallen, as to passing events, and thought that the appointment of a day of general fasting and prayer, would be most likely to call up and alarm their attention.

"No example of such a solemnity had existed since

the days of our distress in the war of '55, since which a new generation had grown up. With the help, therefore, of Rushworth, whom we rummaged over for the revolutionary precedents and forms of the Puritans of that day, preserved by him, we cooked up a resolution, somewhat modernizing their phrases, for appointing the first day of June, on which the post bill was to commence, for a day of fasting, humiliation and prayer, to implore heaven to avert from us the evils of civil war, to inspire us with firmness in support of our rights, and to turn the hearts of the king and parliament to moderation and justice . . .

"We returned home and in our several counties invited the clergy to meet assemblies of the people on the first of June to perform the ceremonies of the day, and to address to them discourses suited to the occasion.

"The people met generally, with anxiety and alarm in their countenances, and the effect of the day, through the whole colony was like a shock of electricity, arousing every man and placing him erect and solidly on his centre. They chose universally, delegates for the convention."

Thus we see that the ministry was not only a great power, but a most welcome factor, in the politics of the infant days of the republic. Mr. Jefferson to the close of his life maintained that preachers, outside of their pulpits, had the right equally with every other citizen, to discuss political questions at will. See letter to Mr. Wendover, dated: Monticello, March 13, 1815, as follows:

". . . I agree, too, that on all other occasions, the preacher has the right, equally with every other citizen, to express his sentiments, in speaking or writing on the subjects of medicine, law, politics, etc., his leisure time being his own, and his congregation not obliged to listen to his conversation or to read his writings; and no one would have regretted more than myself, had any scruple as to the right withheld from us the valuable discourses which have led to the expression of an opinion as to the true limits of the right."

There are other transcripts from Mr. Jefferson which we will furnish our anti-prohibition friends in broken doses during this campaign, but for the present leave them to the operation of the heroic doses already administered.

XII

THAT WHAT-IS-IT?

—oOo—

A LAY SERMON ON THE AUSTIN CALL FOR A CONVENTION

(At Dallas on April 5th—What Was Made Clear and Plain to All.)

TEXT: "Every man hunteth his brother with a net . . . so they wrap it up." Micah 7:2-3.

When an ingenious naturalist found a strange, nondescript animal, so unique as to defy classification he called it

THE WHAT-IS-IT?

When "Uncle Ike," the colored lecturer of White River wanted to be particularly lucid in warning his rapt admirers against any mysterious culinary concoction, his favorite expression was: "You see, my brethren, dis here is an amfibious hermafrodite *species* of de genus omnibus of de soft-shell turtle variety, cause it sets up to have every kind of merit in it from possum and taters to pursimmons and watermillions. But if you darkies is fooled into eating it you'll find it not good for your wholesome. My advice to you niggers is just dis: When you wants possum and taters or pursimmons and watermillions go to de tree whar dey grow and git de real article one at a time whar you *know* it's possum, or taters, or pursimmons, or watermillions and don't you fool your insides wid dis here amfibious hermafrodite species of de genus omnibus of de soft-shell turtle variety."

But the ingenious naturalist and Uncle Ike,

though combining their luminousness might well be startled if, judging by the call they made at Austin, they attempted to classify the convention which is to meet in Dallas on the first Wednesday in April (1887).

The Dallas News well says: "The movement seems to be entirely independent of the whisky interests."

It is the play of Hamlet with Hamlet left out. It seems to be *so* independent of the whisky interests that if you leave out one pale reference in the preamble, which looks like an irrelevant interpolation, no man could conclude from the eight classes invited that "spirituous, vinous or malt liquors" is that "safeguard which the blood and treasure of our ancestors have secured for us," and whose abolition they "are not disposed to tolerate."

That preamble head is entirely unfitted to the eight-class body. One might well imagine that this caller had heard the proclamation made by Jupiter (see Spectator No. 558, 559) and had swapped either head or body with some other convention.

If this unnatural attachment of a whisky head to a pious, patriotic and temperance body was not accidental, then in the language of Micah, "They hunt every man his brother with a net and so they wrap *it up*."

And now let us unwrap the parcel and see what that thing is which is so carefully folded in so many windings of good and variegated cloth. To do this in regular style let us suppose that this parcel so wrapped and so addressed had come by mail for special delivery. The convention postmaster having due regard for his oath of office looks at the curious parcel so carefully folded and reads out loud the address on the outside of the wrapper: *To the follower of Thomas Jefferson who believes with him "that government is best which governs the least."* Whereupon ensued the following colloquy:

1st clerk — "Maybe that package is for Mr.

Barney Gibbs; you know he was in town the other day looking after some interests and told us to forward any mail for him."

2nd clerk—"I say, Mr. Barney Gibbs? why, he is an ex-greenbacker, and was seen several nights ago on the same rostrum with Mr. Arch Cochran, the great follower of Alexander Hamilton, jointly firing off a double-barreled gun at some of the best Jeffersonians in Texas."

3rd clerk—"More likely it's for Col. Thos. R. Bonner, the temporary chairman of the Democratic state convention; he was here at the same time with Mr. Gibbs. Or if the Hon. R. M. Wynn, of Fort Worth, is here, it may be for him; he was the permanent chairman of the state convention."

Postmaster — "This package is meant for somebody who lives in Waco. Here, you parcel boy, take this package to Dr. Thos. Moore, chairman of the Democratic county executive committee."

In due time Dr. Moore receives the package, reads the address and soliloquizes: "Yes! I'm a Jeffersonian, and believe with him that government to be the best which governs least. And as it takes a heap of government to keep men straight where there's no whisky, I naturally suspect this is a bundle of prohibition literature."

He cuts the outside cover, and is startled to find another wrapper bearing this device: "To any man who believes and practices the virtues of temperance, sobriety and moderation, without regard to criminal enactments upon the statute books." "Why," said the startled doctor, "this must be for the temperance society—here, Bart, hand this package to W. D. Jackson."

The great temperance leader receives and opens the package so evidently addressed to his order, but is in turn surprised to find a yet inner wrapper addressed: "To any lover of his country who regards the fundamental principles upon which its government is based as the perfection of human wisdom, and who

— 124 —

is not disposed to tolerate the abolition of any safeguard which the blood and treasure of our ancestors
have secured for us."

The great photographer stands non-plused before
that address. He wrinkles his benign face, puzzled
over the conundrum. "Why," thinks he, "what safeguard is in danger of abolition? This must be an
extract from some old 4th of July oration of a hundred
years ago. I don't know of any safeguard that is in
danger of abolition unless it be a free press muzzled
by a libel law. I think I had better send this package
to the Day office. Maybe Mr. McCollum can make
something out of it."

The twice denuded and yet covered parcel reaches
the Day office, and Mack, after scanning it closely
through his glases, ventures, though in doubt of proper ownership, to unwrap it again; when, behold, like
Dan Rice's shedding showman, it wears, though thrice
unwrapped, an interior suit marked thus:

"To any of the people who believe that the safety and security of our institutions depend upon the
maintenance of perfect individual freedom in all matters of religion, politics and social habits and customs
innocent in themselves and not harmful to others,
and who further believe that the liberty of thinking,
eating, drinking or wearing what we please is not a
'dodge,' but a vital principle, sanctified by centuries
of struggle and consecrated by rivers of blood, never
to be surrendered so long as we claim to be freemen."

For once the Day editor fails to catch on. It
seems to him the most indiscriminate address that
ever came through Uncle Sam's mail bags. In sheer
despair as to where it belongs, he snatches an idea
from the last word "freemen" and sends it post-
haste to the Rev. A. Taylor, colored. Equal to any
emergency, Mr. Taylor cuts the gordian knot, un-
folds the unknown quantity to find himself baffled
by another wrapper having this legend:

"All the people who have not yet lost faith in
the efficacy of the church, the home and the school

in building up and advancing the cause of morality and temperance, and who still believe that these grand agencies, if not diverted from their God-given functions, will always suffice to preserve the morals of our people without the aid of constable or the assistance of spies and informers."

With all readiness to meet the unexpected, Mr. Taylor admits that he has met a "What-is-it?" face to face. Like the others who had in turn killed the hunchback, he determines to leave the mysterious parcel at some man's door. And as Dr. Burleson talks so much of "home," "church" and "school," with his great motto, "Pro Ecclesia Pro Texana," he concluded to put off the package on him, which the venerable college president, so often receiving some book, or piece of scientific apparatus, blandly accepts, then unrolls it to find that ubiquitous inner wrapper this time addressed:

"All patriots who revere the glory and grandeur of our state and the heroism and sacrifice of her sons which have shed a halo of romance over her entire domain, and who are not willing to take any step which may tend to mar its good fellowship and the fraternal love of her sons toward each other or precipitate a dissatisfaction that might end in estrangement of sections and the disruption of the commonwealth."

The amazed doctor imagines that he is reading some fine sentence from Sam Houston's anti-secession speeches, and thinking himself entitled to open anything so vaguely addressed by his old friend, he opens again to be confronted with that ever recurring inside wrapper carefully directed thus:

"All persons who believe that the people of Texas are God-loving and God-fearing people, distinguished as well for their high moral character as for their wisdom in council and their bravery in battle; and those people need no suggestions or advice from alien sources as to how Texas shall manage their own moral and material advancement."

Better satisfied that this is meant for him personally than either of the other addresses, he opens again to see on the neatly folded cover the startling address:

"And finally, all Christian people who believe in the sacred Bible handed down to us by the fathers, for our moral and spiritual guidance and education, and which teaches us in almost its every blessing and vouchsafed us by a merciful God, with a direct indivual responsibility to Him alone for any abuse of His gifts."

The Doctor sees daylight at last. Evidently this is some circular from the Bible Society organized for promoting the love of God's Sacred Scriptures and for disseminating these Holy oracles throughout all nations. In his loyalty to the pastors he is unwilling to intrude into their peculiar church work and so sends Richard with the package over to the Methodist parsonage with the request that Mr. Bishop call in the other resident pastors and open this sacred document.

Receiving the packet, Mr. Bishop, with his usual alacrity summons a pastoral conference, which when assembled, open the now wary and diminished parcel to find a preamble which tells about a meeting at Dallas on the fifth of April, to which all who favor the retention of the liquor traffic are invited. In other and plain words it was a call for an anti-prohibition convention. Simply that and nothing more. Meaning this, and this only, that those who are for whisky, must come up to Dallas to ascertain how to keep it in Texas. And so it was unwrapped.

"Well," says one of the reverend gentlemen, "I don't understand this. This little parcel was addressed to the wrong crowd. I don't see the sense of it."

"But,'" quoth another, "there must be some sense in it for you see it bears the signature of the Hon. George Clark."

"You can't make me believe," replied another, "that George Clark had anything to do with such a roundabout document as that; he is much too sensible a man. Why under that call a couple of thousand prohibitionists could go and capture the whole thing, put in their own chairman and pass a set of ringing temperance resolutions."

"Ah!" cried another, "I have it at last. Eureka! Eureka! You know George Clark is a festive, humorous sort of a man, full of practical jokes. Here is the secret of the thing—look at the date. That '5th' is a typographical error. It means the *first* of April. The whole thing is *an April Fool.*"

Waco, March 31, 1887.

XIII

THE WHISKY ORGAN ANNOUNCES THE DOOM OF LOCAL OPTION

Waco, June 2, 1887.

To the Editor of the Advance:

In to-day's Examiner, the accredited organ of the anti-prohibitionists, is a letter from Jasper county, claiming that the county, which is local option, will go ten to one against state prohibition. The writer, who signs himself "E. I. Kellie," thus voices what he says is the sentiment of the local optionists:

"While they favor local option and have made a success of it, we do not feel that we have any right by our vote to dictate to adjoining counties that they shall not sell liquor. We believe in state rights, county rights, etc."

Upon this remarkable document the Examiner got off the most logical editorial and the most candid that ever to my mind appeared in that paper. After grinding the Jasper county man's logic to fine powder, it says:

"However, we do not cavil at the position assumed by our correspondent. We are not fighting local option now. We are fighting its logical conclusion, state prohibition, and right glad are we to have him help . . . Vote down state prohibition first, and attend to the local option business afterward."

If, after this fair, open warning, the local optionists of Texas are willing to furnish "help" to the anti-prohibitionists, they have not discernment enough to make them accountable beings. Their help is accepted while their reasons for it are justly denounced. And they are coolly, but honestly, informed that their turn comes next.

This is no hasty and irresponsible warning. It is the deliberate declaration of Judge Clark's official anti-prohibition organ. It means just this: "Local option dies with state prohibition. If you local optionists are fools enough to help us kill state prohibition that is well enough, but you must understand that you not only do not purchase our favor but you also prepare the way for your own ruin, and we will ruin you. We'll not fight you now, but will attend to your little business afterward. Verbum Sat."

The Examiner will appreciate our respect for this, the only fair and logical editorial in its columns since it became the anti-prohibition organ, when we assure that paper that its editorial and the Jasper man's letter will be widely circulated by our committee as a campaign document. We will send it to Jasper county and all other local option sections.

The Examiner is right and logical in one point, because it gets hold of one of Senator Coke's right ideas. Senator Coke says, and the Examiner approves:

"Prohibition, or local option, cannot be maintained in the precinct by any argument which is not equally potent to maintain it in the county and in the state and vice versa. . . The argument would seem stronger for the county and still stronger for the state, because of the increased number, and therefore greater good. If good for that precinct, it is better for the county and best for the state." — Interview in the Galveston News, September, 1885.

The logic is invulnerable. The Examiner, with unusual wisdom adds: "If the state has no right to enforce prohibition in counties which do not want it, by the same rule, counties have no right to enforce it in precincts which do not want it, and, of course, it follows clearly and logically, that precincts have no right to force it on an individual who does not want it. This is the whole question in a nutshell."

It is a pleasure to shake hands once with the Examiner. It is a delightful surprise to find logic and candor for once in its columns. It is to be hoped it is not accidental; and fondly hoped that it will not be denied. We commend its logic "in a nutshell" to Barney Gibbs. We specially commend it to its illogical correspondent, Mr. Kellie, and to all Jasper county men. And as company to its open declaration of war against local option, we here conjoin the threat of the Houston Anti-Prohibitionist, which also claims to be the only organ of the liquor men:

"The Prohibitionists are playing with edged tools. If they insist on ramming their extreme measures, as the expression of intolerant opinions, down the throats of the public, they will give birth to a reactionary sentiment that will not stop short of a repeal of the law as it stands, even if the democratic party be shattered in the effort." To which we add a plank from the Chicago Liquor Dealers' convention, October 19, 1886: "We are unalterably opposed to prohibition, whether general or local."

Now, if the Jasper county local optionists want to join this crowd they do it with their eyes open; and we would respectfully address to them some serious questions:

1. If a county has the right to prohibit why has not the state, which is but an aggregate of counties? Is a part greater than the whole?

2. How can Mr. Kellie say that he believes in "state rights" when he denies to it a privilege now enjoyed by any one and every one of its backwoods precincts?

3. If, as the Examiner truthfully and forcefully says, "state prohibition is the logical conclusion" of county local option, how can the logical conclusion be wrong, if the premise is right?

4. If the conclusion is killed, what becomes of the premise? Of what practical value is a cause which is never allowed to produce an effect?

5. If the local optionists fail to make war on their enemies, the liquor-dealers, while they are engaged in a great battle, what reasonable hope can they cherish of maintaining local option, when the triumphant and concentrated enemy masses its vic-

torious columns and millions of money against one little county?

6. If the great ship of state, Prohibition, sinks in this conflict, will not your little boat go down in the vortex?

7. You have saved your county thus far; is it nothing to you that other counties are suffering with this terrible curse as you did once? Will you help to rivet the chains of slavery upon your fellow Texans because you are free? Are you so selfish as to drive the saloons from your county and dump them on other counties, and then vote to keep them there? Is this loving your neighbor as yourself?

8. Have you forgotten that in union there is strength, and that divided we fall? Are you ignorant of the axiom that whatever ceases to grow begins to die? That not to advance means to retreat? That still water stagnates and only running water lives and is pure? Have you not learned in farming that unless you move your fences out you must move them in since undergrowth captures fence-rows and invades the field?

9. Do you not know that when local option joins the liquor dealers against state option that local option digs its own grave, signs its own death warrant and commits suicide?

Let me assure you that the Examiner's open acceptance of your help now and its open threat of tending to your case afterwards means just what an Indian tribe always meant by sending to white settlers a quiver of arrows tied up in a rattlesnake skin, that is, an open declaration of war that was to have no truce and no mercy; it means war to the knife and the knife to the hilt.

Respectfully,

B. H. Carroll,

Chairman Prohibition State General Committee

XIV

A VISION OF AN OLD MAN

(Dr. Carroll in a Speech at Corsicana)

There arises before my mind to-day the vision of an old man, nearly four score years. His head is white as snow and crowned with many honors. He is not far from the day of his death, that sad anniversary of his greatest achievement. The old man looks far back into the past and begins to tell the mournful story of his own eventful life. Let us hear his words. Some of you here to-day were old enough as children to have heard him then when he spoke; all of us can listen now. The old man says:

"Far back in the old colonial days, in 1752, I, a little Virginia boy, only nine years old, was placed in a Latin School where for six years I was instructed in the rudiments of Latin, Greek and French. My teacher, Mr. Douglass, was a clergyman from Scotland. In 1758, I, a lad of seventeen years, entered another school, where for two years I was instructed in the higher classics. My teacher again was a preacher, the Rev. Mr. Maury.

"In 1760, I, a youth of nineteen years, entered William and Mary college, where I was instructed in mathematics, the sciences, ethics, rhetoric and belles lettres. My teacher again was a preacher, Dr. Wm. Small. This preacher fixed the destinies of my life.

"In 1762, I, a young man of twenty-one years, secured through this preacher a place in the law office of Mr. Wythe. In May, 1774, I, as a man thirty-three years old and a member of the Virginia House of Burgesses, learned that the infamous Boston Port Bill would be put in operation in thirty days. We had then no continental congress and no concert of action among the colonies. Our people were enwrapped in lethargy; how could we rouse them?

"I suggested a day of fasting and prayer would be most likely to call up and alarm their attention. The first day of June 1774, the day on which the Port Bill was to commence, was therefore appointed as a day of fasting, humiliation and prayer, to implore heaven to avert from us the evil of civil war, to inspire us in the support of our rights, and to turn the hearts of the king and parliament to moderation and justice. In our several counties we therefore invited the clergy to meet assemblies of the people on the first day of June to perform the ceremonies of the day, and to address to them discourses suited to the occasion. The people met generally with anxiety and alarm in their faces, and the effect of the day through the whole colony was like a shock of electricity, arousing every man and placing him erect and solid on his own center. They chose, universally, delegates for the convention that elected the members of the first continental congress."

Such, gentlemen, as recorded by himself, January 1, 1821, was the old man's soliloquy. It was written at Monticello, Va., and I need not tell you that the old man was Thomas Jefferson, then seventy-seven years old. The men that trained him and the man that, according to his own confession, "probably fixed the destinies of his life," were all preachers.

When the colonies were disunited, when they were steeped in lethargy, when Boston was about to be crushed by that anaconda, the port bill, in such an hour the fathers thought of the preachers. The fathers appealed to the preachers to deliver addresses suitable to the occasions. The preachers responded; the spell of lethargy was broken, and to quote Mr. Jefferson's own words: "The effect of that day through the whole colony was like a shock of electricity." The people were aroused, inspired, and the crisis past, the continental congress was formed.

In that early day that tried men's souls, no man dared rebuke a preacher for discussing the Boston Port Bill. But now, when an enemy more formidable, more relentless and more murderous than Great Britain ever was, already fortified on Texas soil, and bringing by every train foreign money and foreign counsel to rivet upon us the chains of slavery forever — now, when a minister speaks for home and society, the men who most glibly roll the name of Jefferson under their tongue as a sweet morsel — these men shout in madness and frenzy; "Priestcraft! Priestcraft!" and pour out their diatribes of denunciation on church and preacher. There is no Jefferson now to call a day of fasting, humiliation and prayer, whose effect as in that other day, would be like a shock of electricity in arousing and inspiring the people.

XV

PERSONAL LIBERTY

(An address delivered by request in Atlanta, Ga., May 5, 1892, at the Second Baptist Church.)

NOTE: An eye witness states that Dr. Carroll was in excellent trim on this occasion and that his audience was enormous. The price of admission was $.50 but it did not keep the people away. The great audience was swayed by the giant orator like the twigs in the forest are swayed by the breath of the storm. The address was pronounced by all as the ablest effort of the kind ever made in the South.

I count myself happy, ladies and gentlemen, to be thought worthy to speak for such a benevolent purpose, on such a theme, to such an audience. To-morrow the representatives of more than half the Baptists in the world will be assembled in this city to deliberate on measures looking to the redemption of mankind from the spiritual bondage and the sentence of eternal death.

I see the vanguard of that mighty host before me to-night. They are here in the name of him of whom it is written: "If he shall make you free, you shall be free indeed;" of him whose commission was: "To preach deliverance to the captives . . . and to set at liberty them that are bruised."

Back of this host — following such a leader — lie nineteen centuries of history whose every page glows with the record of their unparalleled devotion to both civil and religious liberty. Their pathway through the Dark Ages is luminous with martyr fires. As stranded sea-shells hold forever the ocean songs they caught while resident in the deep, so the scattered stones of ancient dungeons yet retain the echoes of Baptist sighs and groans uttered in hopeless imprisonment for conscience' and for freedom's sake. Their blood, shed by tyrannous persecution, stained Boston Commons in colonial days. It cried out to heaven from the soil of the Old Dominion.

Within six months of the time when Pitcairn's pistol at Lexington opened the Revolutionary War, and almost in sight of Bunker Hill where Warren fell, the choicest spots in the orchards, gardens and farms of a Baptist congregation were auctioned off by the sheriff under a forced and ruinous sale, to provide funds to build a meeting house and to furnish the pastor's salary for another denomination whose families these loyal Baptists had protected with their lives from Indian depredations.

In the early history of this country our people were mainly sturdy sons of agriculture, an occupation which constitutes the basis of all commercial prosperity and healthy national life. When tyranny in any land storms the last retreat of freedom, that final battle field is ever in the rural districts. "Far from the maddening crowd's ignoble strife" it was the pleasing custom of our fathers to meditate upon the unconfined joys of liberty, and to erect her altars on mountain sides and in furrow-scarred valleys.

To their quiet homes she brought her realities instead of the sophisms which too frequently beguile the p o p u l a t i o n of smoke-covered cities. Their hearth-stones were hallowed by her abiding presence. Their cottages, snugly nestling under mountain cliffs or embowered in shady groves, or environed by waving fields of golden grain, have been through the ages her favorite habitat.

To the descendants of such sires personal liberty is a sacred heritage. To speak to them on such a theme, at any time, and anywhere, thrills a speaker's heart and lifts the shadows from his mind. But here, on the centennial of their missionary triumph; here, where they flock in untrammeled thousands to hold untrammeled counsels; here, in this historic town, not now a beleaguered post belted with infantry fire and shaken by the thunders of bombardment; here, not now in ashes over which smokeless chimneys stand as sentinels of desolation in a field of death; but here, in this the foremost city of the New South — the home and also the tomb of Henry W. Grady; here, in a state thick-peopled with the memory of Jesse Mercer and Holcombe and Mell; surely to speak here and now, on such a theme, is inspiration enough to give the tongue the skill which Parrhasius vainly coveted for his pencil the power to paint a martyr's dying groan. The occasion, the presence and the theme deserve a fitting

EXORDIUM.

As such I cite one of the most stirring facts of modern history. On the 28th day of October, 1886, in the New York harbor, was unveiled the gift of France to the United States, Bartholdi's Statue of Liberty Enlightening the World.

It was introduced by a monster parade — civic, municipal, military, naval and diplomatic. The chief officers of this government, official representatives of foreign nations and many of the world's celebrities were proud to participate in the imposing ceremonials of this historic scene.

Back of any such occasion must lie the grand conception of the artist which gave rise to it. And back of his conception must be some great sorrow, the most potent inspiration of genius. And back of the sorrow must exist some sublime and sacred ideal which found expression in his art. The sublime and sacred ideal back of the artist's sorrow was HUMAN LIBERTY, the universal theme of poetry and the ubiquitous genius of patriotism.

The sorrow back of the artist's conception was the ruin of his beloved France, with the Prussian at the gate of Paris, and the iron grasp of Germany on the throat of his native Alsace, "more loyal than the king and more French than Paris." Expatriated by national downfall, Bartholdi's voyage brings him toward the shores of the Western world. When near Bedloe's Island at the entrance of New York Harbor, sadly reading a work of his great compatriot, Victor Hugo, he unconsciously underscored the words: *"This is the angel, liberty; this the light."*

In that hour of sorrow, with that island and harbor before him, filled with memories of the day when the "Lilies of France" and the "Star-Spangled Banner" waved in joint triumph over Cornwallis, making Yorktown the grave of tyranny in the Western world, there and then and thus, that underscored sentence of Victor Hugo suggested the conception of which that statue is the grand consummation.

The sorrows which overwhelmed the Second Republic of France, when Louis Napoleon, by tyrannous *coup d'etat* bound her hand and foot, made Victor Hugo a poet. In his poetic dreams he saw liberty as an Angel and a Light. He told his dream in glowing words. Bartholdi, in his turn, wrapped in the sorrows of the Third Republic, attendant on Prussian occupation, found in the poetic dreams evoked by Hugo's sorrow the suggestion of that Titan Statue, Liberty Enlightening the World. A statue the largest in the world and more famous than that of the Egyptian Pharaohs, of the Ptolemies, at Alexandria, one of the Seven Wonders of ancient times.

Every Youth of America should acquaint himself with the history of that statue, both as to its conception, construction and dedication. It is the fruit of ten years' toil. The very process of construction is most instructive. We see the artist with his small model of clay. Then securing relative proportions by exact measurement, we see the model enlarged. By similar methods another enlargement follows. Then comes the collossal wooden frame and the plaster in the frame. Finally the heavy iron frame itself, embraced as a skin embraces a body, by the sheets of hammered copper.

Every step in construction was according to the

laws of exact science. Every feature conformed to human anatomy. Not only must the relative proportions between the different parts be preserved in each enlargement, but every precaution known to human science had to be employed to secure perpetuity. It had to be guarded against the decay of material and shielded against the lightning stroke. It must be so built as to defy alike the corroding tooth of time and the sweep of Atlantic storms. It must be guarded against the alternate contraction of cold and expansion of heat.

And there, as a triumph of engineering and scientific skill, it has stood immovable. Winters have robed her from head to foot in garments of ice, with icicles dependent from her very torch. Hoar frost has breathed with the chill of death between the joints of her harness. Summer in her turn has beat with ruthless heat on her unsheltered head, making the copper scales a sheath of fire. The storm-king has marshalled the winds of heaven from every point of the compass and swept with sudden dash or howling hurricane against her. The angry ocean has blustered and foamed about her. Darkness has tried to put out her light. But there she stands without weariness. Time writes no wrinkles on the serenity of her brow. Age does not stoop her form nor decrepitude weaken her limbs. Darkness never dims her light. Silent as the Sphinx, immovable as the Pyramids, she does not speak; she *shines*.

See this statue tower one hundred and fifty-one feet above its pedestal, itself one hundred and fifty feet high; realize by measurement the colossal proportions disguised in symmetry. Upon that uplifted torch, twelve men can stand. The toe equals a man in length. The nose is three feet, nine inches long. The forefinger is seven feet, eleven inches long. The eye widens twenty-eight inches. The whole statue weighs 440,000 lbs. — equal to the great bell of Moscow, which no man was ever able to hang. It cost $250,000. It was shipped by sections in 300 cases.

There it stands on Bedloe Island. The head is crowned. The right hand upholds the torch. The left hand embraces a tablet inscribed, "July 4, 1776." It is lighted by electricity, and while the torch itself is concealed by an arrangement of reflectors the sky above is illuminated up to the stars. The face is wrapped in a silver halo like the face of Moses fresh from God's presence, and the tablet glows like the tables of stone inscribed by the finger of deity on Sinai. The statue fronts all coming fleets and the perilous sea and looks lovingly towards far off France, the donor. Such a statue might well inspire Whittier's poem:

THE STATUE OF LIBERTY

The land that from the rule of Kings
  In freeing us itself made free,
Our Old World sister to us brings
  Her sculptured dream of liberty.

Unlike the shapes on Egypt's sands,
  Uplifted by the toil-worn slave,
On freedom's soil, with freemen's hands
  We rear the symbol free hands gave.

O France, the beautiful, to thee
  Once more a debt of love we owe —
In peace beneath thy FLEUR DE LIS,
  We hail a later Rochambeau.

Rise, stately symbol, holding forth
  Thy light and hope to all who sit
In chains of darkness. Belt the earth
  With watch-fires from thy torch uplift.

Reveal the primal mandate still,
  Which chaos heard and ceased to be,
Trace on mid air the eternal will,
    In signs of fire "Let man be free."

Shine far, shine free, a guiding light
To reason's way and virtue's aim;
A lightning flash the wretch to smite
Who shields his crimes with thy
bless'd name.

The statue in its conception, material, construction, beauty and design is a type of all true liberty. Freedom is the child of sorrow and sacrifice and law. There must be just proportions in all its parts. The constituent elements must have no decaying or corroding material. Liberty is an Angel; Liberty is Light.

Anything unscientific in structure, anything impure or corrupting, anything non-luminous, which claims to be liberty is an impostor and a fraud. But to all light there is a background of darkness; to every substance, a shadow; to the best coin a counterfeit.

From my youth I have loved liberty as the child of the skies. Her champions have been my heroes. The battle fields crimsoned with the blood of her martyrs have in all their history been as familiar to me as household words. With the Peri of ancient legend, I once fondly but vainly supposed that patriot blood would even open the gates of Paradise, and with her said:

"Oh, if there be on this earthly sphere,
A boon, an offering heaven holds dear,
'Tis the last libation that Liberty draws
From the heart that bleeds and breaks
in her cause."

With such thoughts, in my boyhood, have I stood within the walls of the Alamo in San Antonio, and fancied I saw before me the heroic band of Travis

— 142 —

perish — one by one — to the last man — Travis, Crockett, Bowie — all lie down in bloody death, heaped about by their slaughtered enemies.

Accompanying this love of liberty was ever an undying hatred of its counterfeit. With Madame Roland, I have often exclaimed: "O Liberty, what crimes are perpetrated in thy name!" Some years ago while pondering in bitterness of spirit the many iniquities that have sheltered themselves under the skirt of her mantle, my eyes chanced to fall on a picture in the illustrated Texas Siftings representing Bartholdi's Statue of Liberty, so wondrously beautiful in itself, contrasted with its own horrible and sinister shadow. I was amazed that two things so like, could be so unlike. Gazing steadfastly and meditatively on that direful shadow, an instructive lesson impressed itself on my mind. The statue represented genuine liberty. The shadow, its base counterfeit. With the lesson came a purpose. I took the picture to a gifted artist and said, "Put this on canvass for me. Enlarge it into a huge cartoon." He has done his work well. I have it here. Let us unroll the canvass and take a look at his work.

Ladies and gentlemen, behold the picture! (Here the speaker pulled a string and unrolled a cartoon before the audience. It represented Bartholdi's Statue of Liberty standing in the foreground. In the background was a horrid shadow which must be seen to be appreciated.)

Ladies and gentlemen, behold the cartoon! "Look on this picture, then on that." Mark the contrast between the statue and the shadow. You see this shining crown on Liberty's head. Behold on the shadow it is the head-dress of the furies. Each tapering crown-point on the one has become a writhing, fiery serpent on the other. The torch in Liberty's hand sends up to heaven and out to sea a steady gleam of light.

The torch of the shadow is lurid, wavering and smoke-mingled, suggesting arson and conflagration.

The gleam of the one is like the smile of an angel seen through a vista of stars; the light of the other is like the flash of a distiller's furnace, glaring through a fissure in the pit. The tablet clasped in Liberty's left hand, and inscribed with the date of the nation's birth, becomes in the clutch of the shadow a tombstone on which no man will dare to write an epitaph. The face of the statue is the visage of an angel, while that of the shadow is the visage of Hecate or of that Medusa whose horrid look turned beholders to stone, or some of those images of despair which peopled Dante's Inferno, and immortalized the pencil of Dore.

THE OBJECT OF THE CARTOON.

It is designed by this object lesson to make the eye see the argument addressed to the ear, so that through the gate-way of two senses instead of one the important lessons of the theme may be imparted.

Now to the application: There is such a thing as personal liberty. It is an inalienable and inestimable blessing. There is such a thing as licentiousness. It is an unspeakable curse. The one genders to life, the other to death. One is angelic, the other demoniacal. One is light, the other conflagration. And yet one bears the semblance of the other. It wears the clothes of the other. It assumes the voice of the other. There cannot be named a form of licentiousness, no matter how debasing, corrupt, soul-destroying that has not said of itself: "I am PERSONAL LIBERTY."

It has claimed all the honors, affected all the sanctity and worn all the laurels of Personal Liberty. It has sheltered behind Liberty's bulwarks, plundered its revenues, poured out filthy libations on its altars and defiled its holy temples with beastly orgies. The label of personal liberty has been pasted on anarchy, thefts, murder, lust, arson, and all unrighteousness

of trade. The smuggler, the pimp and the gambler,
the drunkard and the one who makes him drunk —
all human birds of prey, blasphemously take her name
upon their lips.

The condemned anarchists in Chicago called it
personal liberty to threaten a Metropolis with ruin.
The punishment of their crimes they styled tyranny.
The infatuated girl who sought to wed August Spies
in the shadow of the gallows, called him her *hero*,
and linked his name with Kosciusko. Well might
Whittier in his last couplet call upon the light from
Liberty's torch to be:

"A lightning's flash the wretch to smite,
Who shields his crimes with thy bless'd name."

In the necessary war between society and licentiousness it is the part of wisdom to foreknow the
issues on which opposing parties will most probably
align their forces to anticipate the strategies of an
artful and formidable adversary. All experience
teaches that a cause which cannot rely on its own
merits, must seek alliance with better things and
divert attention from its iniquities by fictitious or
irrevelant issues. Evil would be without enthusiasm
and without respectable advocates, on an issue of
avowed evil. Necessity requires it to adopt a watchword, potent, magical. That watchword is, "Personal
Liberty."

All history leads to this solemn conclusion:
When society attempts to put the restraints of law
on any giant evil, then you rouse the demagogue.
You unseal a volcano. You jeopardize your life. The
land is filled with howlings:

"PERSONAL LIBERTY IS ENDANGERED."

The reason for adopting the line of defence suggested by this slogan lies in the fact that the name
of liberty is sacred with all people. Its memories

create eloquence. Its generalities shelter sophisms.
Its appeals to grateful patriotism come with all the
sanction of historic names: Washington, Wallace
and Marion. Having adopted such line of defence,
by similar sophistry, the opposing line of offence
must be weakened. It becomes necessary to mini-
mize and degrade the term, "General Welfare." It
is nicknamed the "General Welfare Dodge." And
so discrimination is lost in the fogs of passion and
the mystifications of declamation.

Yet, let me assure you, all who love your country:
The salvation of this Republic depends upon discriminating between liberty and licentiousness. For this
discrimination, God of our Country, give us clearness
of vision, then courage to promote the one and restrain the other.

Therefore, loving my country as I do, loving
liberty as the child of God, I do, here and now, indict
any form of licentiousness that masquerades in the
garb of liberty as an imposture, as a ravening wolf
in sheep's clothing, as a deadly peril to society. That
shadow is its portrait. In the name of the inscription on the tablet in Liberty's hand and the tombstone
without an epitaph in the talons of yonder demon, I
impeach it as a wrecker's beacon lighting storm-
driven vessels to shipwreck and their unhappy crews
to plunder and murder.

I denounce it as Medusa, as Hecate, as devilish
and sensual, not angelic, as perishable in element,
unscientific in structure, as non-luminous in every
saving sense. I denounce it as the mover of storms
and the provocation of lightnings. Back of its conception is the lust of avarice and appetite. Back of
the lust is enmity to God and man. For true liberty,
represented by that luminous and angelic statue, men
have willingly died or patiently sighed away their
souls in dark dungeons, or borne, in hope of redemption, the manacles riveted by tyranny.

But men have not so suffered and died for that
shadow. You remember Francis Marion in the

swamps talking to the British officer of his sweetheart, *Liberty,* and living therefore on roasted potatoes; and you see that same Marion crushing with an iron hand the grog-shops and bawdy-houses which threaten to undermine the foundation of liberty. What men have not fought for, let R. J. Burdette tell:

"My dear boy, men have fought, bled and died, but not for beer. Arnold Winkelried did not throw himself upon the Austrian spears because he was ordered to close his saloon at 9 o'clock. William Tell did not hide an arrow under his vest because the edict had gone forth that the free-born Switzer should not drink a keg of beer every Sunday. Freedom did not shriek as Kosciusko fell over a whisky barrel. Warren did not die that beer might flow as the brooks murmur seven days a week. Even the battle of Brandywine was not fought that whisky might be free. No clause in the Declaration of Independence declares that a Sunday concert garden, with five brass horns and 100 kegs of beer, is the inalienable right of a free people and the cornerstone of good government.

"Tea, mild, harmless, innocent tea, the much sneered at temperance beverage, the feeble drink of effeminate men and good old women, holds a higher place; it fills a brighter, more glorious page; it is a grander figure in the history of this United States, than beer. Men liked tea, my boy, but they hurled it into the sea in the name of liberty, and they died rather than drink it until they made it free. It seemed to be worth fighting for and the best men in the world fought for it. The history of the United States is incomplete with tea left out. As well might the historian omit Faneuil Hall and Bunker Hill, as tea. But there is no story of heroism or patriotism with rum for its hero.

"The battles of this world, my son, have been fought for grander things than free whisky. The heroes who fall in the struggles for rum, fall shot in the neck, and their martyrdom is clouded by the haunting phantoms of the jim-jams. Whisky makes men fight, it is true, but they usually fight other drunken men. The champion of beer does not stand in the temple of fame, but he stands in the police court. Honor never has the *delirium tremens*. Glory does not wear a red nose, and fame blows a horn but never takes one."

In the language of a Texas Senator: "I take it to be an axiomatic truth that liberties of a people is a subject upon which there can be no trifling. We must be grave, we must be considerate, we must be sagacious. We must put the best foot foremost, we must make no mistake."

As a safeguard against mistakes we need, first of all, *clear and accurate definitions.* Then

What mean the terms employed?

What is personal liberty?

What is general welfare?

What are their relations to each other?

What is the origin, and what the object of government?

On this necessity of definition, hear that famous heathen, Marcus Aurelius Antonius: "Make for thyself a definition or description of the thing which is presented to thee, so as to see distinctly what kind of a thing it is in its substance, in its nudity, in its complete entirety, and tell thyself its proper name, and the names of the things of which it has been compounded and into which it will be resolved. For nothing is so productive of elevation of mind as to be able to examine methodically and truly every object which is presented to thee in life, and always to look at things so as to see at the same time what kind of a universe this is, and what kind of use everything performs in it, and what value everything has with reference to the whole, and what with reference to man, who is a citizen of the highest city of which all other cities are like families."

Mr. Sharswood, author of the Notes on Blackstone's Commentaries, says: "Liberty is a word, which it is of the utmost importance to mankind that they should clearly comprehend, for though a genuine spirit of liberty is the noblest principle that can animate the heart of man, yet liberty in times has been the clamor of men of profligate lives and desperate fortunes." See Sharswood's Blackstone, 126.

Another distinguished writer has said: "It is a common fault with enthusiasts for liberty that they do not clearly define what it is they would make free. . . . There are some things which cannot be liberated too much; and there are some things which devour all rational and enriching liberty, if they are not effectually tied up; and partisans of liberty who are so blindly its partisans that they will not discriminate, will not organize a means to liberate what is really liberal and find what makes a vicious and destructive bondage, are its partisans without being its promoters."

For correct definitions we do not appeal to speculative doctrinaires like Herbert Spencer. In his "Social Statics" he defines government as "voluntary association for mutual protection" (page 303) and characterizes it as a "necessary evil" (page 25) and as "essentially immoral" (page 230) and denies the right of the state to educate (page 361) or to impose "sanitary inspection" (page 406).

In opposition to this it is claimed that government is of divine origin (Romans 13:1-7). And in this fact lies the higest motive which can influence man to reverence and obey it. It is further claimed that government is a righteous necessity arising from the moral and social character of man and the common brotherhood of the race. It cannot therefore be essentially evil and immoral. In fact when the idea of God is not left out, essential evil and immorality is an impossible conception. Nor is mutual protection the whole design of government. Nor is the government a mere voluntary association. Nor does the necessity for government decrease as civilization increases. The contrary is true, for civilization increases the relations between men and makes those relations more complex. Mr. Huxley has been quoted as describing Herbert Spencer's speculations on this point as "administrative nihilism."

For clear ideas of government and correct definitions of the terms, "personal liberty" and "general welfare," let us appeal to universally accepted authorities.

Blackstone, this standard author, says: "The principal aim of society is to protect individuals in the enjoyment of those absolute rights which were vested in them by the immutable laws of nature, but which could not be preserved in peace without that mutual assistance and intercourse which is gained by the institution of friendly and social institutions. Such rights as are social and RELATIVE result from and are posterior to the formation of states and societies. Therefore, the principal view of human law is, or ought always to be, to explain, protect and enforce such rights as are absolute, which are in themselves few and simple, and then such rights as are relative, which arising from a variety of connections, will be far more numerous and complicated."

To show the limit of human law, and how what he here calls absolute rights must be, in society, subordinated to relative rights, he says: "Let a man, therefore be ever so abandoned in his principles, or vicious in his practices, provided he keeps his wickedness to himself, and does not offend against the rules of public decency, he is out of the reach of human law. But if he makes his vices public though they be such as seem principally to affect himself (as drunkenness, or the like), then they become by the bad example they set of pernicious affects to society; and, therefore, it is then the business of human laws to correct them. Here the circumstance of publication is what alters the nature of the case. PUBLIC sobriety is a relative duty, and therefore enjoined by our laws: private sobriety is an absolute duty, which, whether it be performed or not, human tribunals can never know and therefore they can never enforce it by any civil sanction."

The learned author then continues: "The absolute rights of men considered as a free agent, endowed with discernment to know good from evil, and with power of choosing those measures, which appear to him to be the most desirable, are usually summed up in one general appelation, and denominated the natural liberty of mankind. This natural liberty consists properly in a power of acting as one thinks fit, without any restraint or control, unless by the laws of nature; being a right, inherent in us by birth, and one of the gifts of God to man at his creation, when he endowed him with the faculty of free will. But every man, when he enters into society, as the price of so valuable a purchase, and in consideration of receiving the advantages of mutual commerce, obliges himself to conform to those laws, which the community has thought proper to establish."

Having thus defined "natural liberty" the author proceeds: "Political, therefore, or civil liberty, which is that of a member of society, is no other than natural liberty so far restraining by human laws (and no farther) as is necessary and expedient for the general advantages of the public. Hence we may collect that the law, which restrains a man from doing mischief to his fellow citizens though it diminishes the natural, increases the civil liberty of mankind."

He further adds: "So that laws, when prudently formed, are by no means subversive, but rather introductive, of liberty; for as Mr. Locke has well observed, *where there is no law there is no freedom*. But then, on the other hand, that constitution or frame of government, that system of laws, is alone calculated to maintain civil liberty, which leaves the subject the entire master of his own conduct, except in those points wherein the public good required some direction or restraint."

Upon these paragraphs, Mr. Sharswood, chief-justice of the supreme court of Pennsylvania, and author of the notes to the edition of Blackstone, from which I quote, says: "This section is one of the very few intelligible descriptions of liberty which has hitherto been communicated to the world. Though declamation and eloquence in all ages have exhausted their stores upon this favorite theme, yet reason has made so little progress in ascertaining the nature and boundaries of liberty, that there are very few authors indeed, either of this or of any other country, who can furnish the studious and serious reader with a clear and consistent account of this idol of mankind. . . . THE LIBERATAS QUIDLIBET FACIENDI, or the liberty of doing everything which a man's passions urge him to attempt or his strength enables him to effect, is savage ferocity; it is the liberty of a tiger and not the liberty of a man."

Let us pause here to impress upon the mind some reflections suggested by these definitions:

1.   God, the creator, is the author of human government which therefore rests upon the immutable, natural laws, implying a fixed and antecedent standard of right and wrong.

2.   Man by his moral and social nature was designed for society. The social is his normal condition. When in an isolated or savage state he is at war with his nature.

3.   Hence, association with his fellow men is not strickly speaking, a voluntary matter with him; *when he disssociates, he sins.*

4.   Even when considered by himself his absolute rights are limited by immutable, natural laws. Even his natural liberty is not "savage ferocity," nor the "liberty of a tiger."

5.   That where there is no law there is no freedom. Laws are not subversive of liberty but introduce it.

6. Natural and civil liberty are not contradictory in essence, but essentially the same. The decrease of natural liberty by proper legal restraints, increases it under the name of civil liberty.

7. That the vicious are accustomed to invoke the name of liberty as a cover for their evil deeds.

But continuing the authorities, I read from Kent's Commentaries on American Law, Vol. II. On the first page he thus defines civil liberty: "It consists in being protected and governed by laws made or assented to, by the representatives of the people, and conducive to the general welfare."

On page 340 he says: "The government may, by general regulations, interdict such uses of property as would create nuisances, and become dangerous to the lives or health, or peace or comfort of the citizens. Unwholesome trades, slaughter houses, operations offensive to the senses, the deposit of powder, the application of steam power to propel cars, the building with combustible materials, and the burial of the dead may all be interdicted by law, in the midst of dense masses of population, on the general and rational principle that every person ought so to use his property as not to injure his neighbors and that private interests must be made subservient to the general interests of the community."

Let us not leave out such an authority as John Stuart Mill on the principles involved. On the 20th page, after stating the object of his essay to be the assertion of one simple principle, he thus defines the principle: "That principle is, that the sole end for which mankind warranted, individually or collectively, an interfering with the liberty of action of any of their number is SELF PROTECTION. That the only purpose for which power can be rightfully exercised over any member of a civilized community against his will, IS TO PREVENT HARM TO OTHERS."

On the 125th page where he is endeavoring to ascertain the rightful limit to the sovereignty of the individual and just where the authority of society commences, he says: "To individuality should belong the part of life in which it is chiefly the individual that is interested to society, the part which chiefly interests society."

On the 123rd page, after discussing some individual action which society should not touch he adds: "It is far otherwise if he has infringed the rules necessary for the protection of his fellow-creatures, individually or collectively. The evil consequences of his acts do not then fall on himself, but on others; and society, as the protector of all its members, must retaliate on him; must inflict pain on him for the express purpose of punishment, and must take care that it be sufficiently severe."

On the 137th page he sums up the matter thus: "Whenever, in short, there is definite damage, or a definite risk of damage, either to an individual or to the public, the case is taken out of the province of liberty and placed in that of morality of law."

On the 158th page he continues: "Trade is a social act. Whoever undertakes to sell any description of goods to the public, does what affects the interests of other persons, and society in general; and this conduct, in principle, comes within the jurisdiction of society."

So far as the principles are concerned I could not get them more clearly before you if I quoted the whole book. Upon just such principles the prohibition of any social evil rests its cause and founds its hopes. In these principles it finds a refuge from slander and a refutation of the charge that it invades personal liberty.

Let us apply these principles to a specific business: The liquor traffic as a trade comes within the jurisdiction of society. As it not merely conveys "a definite threat of damage" but actually "inflicts a definite damage," it is, according to Mr. Mill, taken out of the province of liberty and placed in that of Morality and law. It is, therefore, worthy of severe punishment at the hands of society, which justifies its interference on the acknowledged ground of harm to others. Of course, Mr. Mill makes no such application of his principles. He denies that this particular trade should be taken out of the province of liberty. For his principles we have respect; for his opinions as to their application, none whatever.

In making his application he becomes irrational, inconsistent and at war with his own principles. Take a few samples: He regards prohibitory liquor laws, the prohibition of the importation of opium into China, the restrictions on the sale of poisonous drugs (page 159), interference with Mormonism on the ground of bigamy (page 153), restrictions on fornication and gambling (page 165), all sabbatarian laws (page 151), and stringent divorce laws (page 173), all opposed to personal liberty, and as an invasion of it, unjustifiable upon the part of the state. He quotes approvingly another author that "Marriage should be dissolved at the option of either party."

He then gravely tells us that to prevent young people from marrying unless the man can show to society that he is able to support a wife is not an invasion of personal liberty (page 171). While he regards it as in accord with personal liberty for a man to sell himself into degradation and ruin as a drunkard, yet it is opposed to personal liberty to allow him to sell himself as a slave to work for another (page 171). While he would make gambling, drunkenness, and fornication free from all restriction, he justifies the punishment of pimps and the suppression of gambling houses (pages 165, 166) but does not justify the suppression of the dram shop. The freedom that he justifies in some of his applications is of a kind if not degree with the freedom clamored for by all profligates, free-lovers, anarchists, and Sabbath-breakers. The limit they seek is to be free from God, from marriage, from law, from all things good.

In the language of inspiration: "While they promise them liberty, they themselves are the servants of corruption; for of whom a man is overcome, of the same is he brought in bondage." As throwing far clearer light upon both the principles and applications involved in this controversy, I introduce the testimony of

VICTOR HUGO.

He says in his book, entitled, "93," and on the 148th page: "The French Convention promulgated this grand axiom: 'The liberty of each citizen ends where the liberty of another citizen commences,' which comprises in two lines all human social law. It declared indigence sacred; it declared infirmity sacred in the blind, and the deaf, and the dumb, who became wards of the State; maternity sacred in the girl-mother whom it consoled and lifted up; infancy sacred in the orphan, whom it caused to be adopted by the country; innocence sacred in the accused who when acquitted was indemnified.

"It branded the slave trade; it abolished slavery; it proclaimed civic joint-responsibility; it decreed gratuitous instruction; it organized national education by the normal school of Paris, central schools in the chief towns, primary schools in communes. It created the academies of music and the museums, it decreed the unity of the code; the unity of weights and measures, and the unity of calculation by the decimal system. It established the finances of France, and caused the public credit to succeed to the long monarchial bankruptcy.

"It put the telegraph in operation; to old age it gave endowed almshouses; to sickness, purified hospitals; to instruction, the Polytechnic school; to science, the Bureau of Longitudes; to human intellect, the Institute. At the same time that it was national, it was cosmopolitan. Of the eleven thousand, two hundred and ten decrees which emanated from the convention, a third had a political aim, two-thirds a human aim. It declared universal morality the basis of society, and the universal conscience the basis of law."

On this most remarkable paragraph in European Literature I desire to make the following comments: Better than any other passage known to me it illustrates the boundaries between "Personal Liberty" and the "General Welfare." Not one of the great remedial and reformatory measures cited but was an infringement of the individual man's *natural* liberty.

Take for instance the public schools. I have heard distinguished men say that the public school system was an invasion of personal liberty; that the plain English of it was, "Taking money out of one man's pocket to educate another man's children." And, certainly every argument against the abolition of any evil traffic, predicated on personal liberty, applies with ten fold power against the public schools and yet our public schools constitute our glory. No man could live before the people and denounce them.

BILL OF RIGHTS AND THE JUDICIARY.

In ascertaining the limits of personal liberty as restrained by the general welfare, we need to consider only one other legal question. It has been alleged, and truly, that majorities, through legislative enactment may make a tyrant of the statute book and thereby oppress the minority, in matters of personal liberty. But it cannot be alleged that our fathers have not guarded against such a contingency. What then is the bulwark against majority tyranny? What is it then that effectually prevents our people from magnifying the "General Welfare" into such proportions that personal or civil liberty will be swallowed up entirely? Let the authorities speak once more upon this point.

Mr. Sharswood in his notes in Blackstone says: "The Constitution of the United States and the constitution of the several states are accompanied with 'Bills of Rights,' which are intended to declare and set forth the restrictions which the people in their sovereign capacity have imposed upon their agents — various governments established by these Constitutions. But as the persons composing the different branches of these governments are chosen directly or indirectly, by a majority of the people these provisions of the Bills of Rights are really RESTRICTIONS IMPOSED UPON THESE MAJORITIES. They constitute the security of the individual members of society against the acts of the majority. The great bulwark of the reserved rights protected by these restrictions is the JUDICIARY DEPARTMENT. They have the unquestioned power of declaring any act of government in any of its departments, which infringes any of these rights, to be utterly null and void. That department spreads the broad and impregnable shield of its protection over the life, limbs, reputation, liberty and property of the citizen, when invaded by the will of the majority." See notes in Sharswood's Blackstone, pages 124, 125.

Here, then as upon an eternal Gibraltar, we rest the merits of this question. That Bill of Rights contains all of the reserved liberty of the citizen, which even majority legislation may not touch. Moreover the determining of just what is the meaning and scope of the Bill of Rights has been exclusively confided to the Supreme Court. From their decision there is no appeal but revolution.

But to pass from the abstract to the concrete we inquire, Has this question of the violation of fundamental rights by prohibtory legislation been tested, and thoroughly tested? Have appeals predicated on the Bill of Rights been carried to the Supreme Court for decision? If so, what has been that decision?

Here I will introduce as an authoritative witness, Thomas M. Cooley, formerly a justice of the Supreme Court of Michigan, and Jay, Professor of Law in the University of Michigan. In his treatise on Constitutional Limitations, a universally accepted authority, he tells us that: "Those laws which undertake altogether to prohibit the manufacture and sale of intoxicating drinks as a beverage have been assailed . . . as subversive of fundamental rights, and therefore not within the grant of legislative powers."

Then the author shows by decisions, too numerous for citation here, that the court invariably held that such legislation was valid and not subversive of any man's personal liberty. Notably, the one in 5th Howard (pages 504, 633). What the Supreme Court of the U. S. has decided on such appeals predicated upon those amendments to the Federal Constitution, which embody the National Bill of Rights, the Supreme Courts of the several States have also decided in all cases of appeal, based upon the Bill of Rights adopted by these States. Within my knowledge no appeal from such legislation based on personal liberty has ever been sustained by any Supreme Court whether State or National.

To recapitulate: We have sought in the highest standards a definition of the term, "Personal liberty." We have found that such liberty must be either natural or civil. Following the suggestion of Marcus Aurelius Antonius we have, from the most authoritative sources, made for ourselves a definition of liberty, both natural and civil. We have seen distinctly what kind of a thing it is in substance, in its nudity and in its entirety. We have seen of what it is compounded and into what it will be resolved. We have seen what uses it performs with reference to the universe and to man. Then we have seen that the prohibition of licentiousness of any kind and every evil traffic, has been tried, as to this definition, time and time again and upon all points, before the highest judicial tribunals. And that the decisions have been numerous and univocal. That they all declare that such legislation is not an invasion of liberty. Hence it follows that any use or application of the term, personal liberty, outside of the limitations of these definitions and decisions is purely arbitrary and violative of the established meaning of words.

Such, ladies and gentlemen, are the authorities. Their bare citation is an unanswerable argument for prohibition of any evil which menaces society. It would violate all the authorities, all facts and common sense, to assume that no personal liberty is to be surrendered to the general welfare. Then if some must be surrendered, What and how much? are the vital questions. Evidently that, however much, which threatens the existence of society and government.

Thus is the whole matter narrowed by inexorable logic, down to this issue: Is any form of evil, as it now exists, sufficiently corrupting and detrimental to the general welfare to warrant its abatement as a nuisance? If it be so, then to abate it does not invade personal liberty but increases civil liberty. The whole and only controversy thus becomes a question of fact. The only burden of proof resting upon those favoring its abatement is to establish this fact. The only ground of defense left to those opposing abatement is to show that license of the evil secures the same great end in a better way. The controversy then is: Prohibition in full, or partial prohibition by a revenue-producing license.

But remember when you license an evil for revenue, you virtually endorse it. You become a partner in it. To regain this revenue the traffic resorts to adulteration, fraud and extortion, To protect itself it enters politics. It bids for ignorant, vicious and purchasable votes. It dominates in primaries and dictates nominations in conventions. It silences the police. It suborns evidence. It bribes juries and judges. It lobbies the legislatures. It combines with all kindred evils. It seeks the balance of power. Its own forces are as compact as a Roman legion or a Macedonian phalanx. It holds the axe of execution over the head of the politician. He knows he takes his political life in his hands when he opposes it. It is a secret tribunal. It is an owl of the night. It acknowledges no criterion but success and worships no God but self-interest. It has no patriotism and carries the black flag.

Instance the shameful record of the Louisiana Lottery. What that lottery was for a time, the liquor traffic is all the time. Who can outline this traffic? To-day we see it in perspective, as it throws across the deep and distant heavens, against a back-ground tragic and terrible, its direful and ever changing profile, a gnomic tribunal, a Titan fighter, an athlete, a brooder, a vampire, an octopus, a python, a volcano.

It has the stealth of the tiger, the bound of the panther, the weight of the mastodon, the momentum of an avalanche, and the speed of lightning. Terrible in its secretiveness, it never foretells what it wants nor where it goes nor when it strikes. The rattlesnake is more merciful. This thing advances and recoils. It threatens North and strikes South. With one fringe of its cloud it eclipses the genius of S. S. Prentiss, while with a paralyzing glare of its lightning it "turns the poesy of Burns into a tuneless babble." As was said of a French communist: "Wherever it respires it conspires." With no more conscience than cold iron, no more heart than an iceberg, it confronts us to-day, as ever before, always the foe of man, always inexorable, inaccessible, glacial.

The man who makes friends with it lashes himself to a tomb, with the boom of eternity's retribution sounding in his ears. The party which makes coalition with it invokes the scorn of man and invokes the judgment of God. If you ask the centuries what is the result of this traffic, the answer comes century by century, like the peal of minute guns from some drowning ship, or like the measured stroke of a funeral bell, or like the storm-thud of the surge on granite shores: "Death — ever death — utter death," an eternal reverberation which fills all history. Remember all this when you favor partial restriction by license instead of total restriction by prohibition.

We have not now to prove that legislation on such subjects is proper. That is already settled by multiform legislation in every land. We have not now to prove that *prohibitory* legislation is right, for that is settled by the authorities which declare that restrictive legislation is prohibitory. We have not now to inquire whether state prohibition makes a tyrant of the statute book, and invades the reserved, fundamental rights of the citizen, for the only authority competent to decide that question has already affirmed in decisions of the Supreme Court that such legislation is in harmony with the Bill of Rights and does not infringe the reserved rights of the citizen.

We have not now to disprove, where trade is involved, that such legislation invades personal liberty on the ground that it affects the buyer and not the seller. For this objection is equally strong against all sanitary laws, all revenue laws, and has been declared by the highest authority without any weight. We have not now to pause before such gloomy questions as this: If the prohibition of one evil prevails, when and where will such legislation stop?

The one and universal answer is, the Bill of Rights, interpreted by the Supreme Court is the bulwark against extremes. Men can have no better. From such decisions there is no appeal but revolution, and no law can guard against absolute revolution. But we have a right to ask that the law may not protect evil. When it does it must separate from God: "Shall the throne of iniquity have fellowship with thee, which frameth mischief by a law?"

We have a right to demand that the government shall not be a partner in any evil. It should not sell indulgences. We want Uncle Sam and every State and city to dissolve partnership, come out of such business, wash their hands and put on clean clothes. We have a right to protest against the regulation of evil by law. It is the function of government to prohibit and condemn but not to condone crime. We have a right to demand that the government shall not, while prohibiting little sins, allow the greatest crimes to go free.

"Will you the felon fox restrain,
And yet take off the tiger's chain?"

Will you condemn the mad-dog to summary death for fear of hydrophobia and not crush the serpent whose bite produces delirium tremens and *mania a potu*?

Will you suppress obscene literature, gambling houses, lotteries and counterfeiting, and let this traffic go free?

If you would spread over it the aegis of law, if you would thus make it legal to establish "an organized hunt after men's souls," if you would enter into a partnership with such a death-producing, slavery-engendering traffic, then for the sake of righteousness and truth, DO NOT THIS THING IN THE NAME OF LIBERTY. The children of liberty must have virtue and intelligence.

The state needs order and not anarchy. It needs men, great men and good men, or it will die. Licentiousness produces not such men. They must be men of sobriety to be the children of liberty. Of such men spoke Sir William Jones:

"What constitutes a state?
Not high-rais'd battlement or labored mound,

Thick wall or moated gate;
Not cities proud with spires and turrets crowned;
Not bays and broad-arm'd ports,
Where laughing at the storm, rich navies ride;
Not sparr'd and spangl'd courts,
Where low-browed baseness wafts perfume to pride.
No; men, high-minded men
With powers as far above dull brutes endued
In forest, brake or den,
As beasts excel cold rocks and brambles rude;
Men who their duties know,
But know their rights and knowing dare maintain,
Prevent the long-aimed blow,
And crush the tyrant, while they rend his chain,
These constitute a State.

XVI

PROHIBITION

(Texas Baptist Standard, June 13, 1895.)

Waco, Texas, June 7, 1895.

W. S. Blackshear,
Chairman Prohibition County Committee.

Dear Sir and Friend: —

It affords me pleasure to reply to your favor, June 6, referring to inquiries in regard to my silence in the pending Prohibition Campaign and inviting an expression of my views thereon.

Considering my relation to a former county canvass, and particularly my advocacy of prohibition, in the State Campaign of 1887, my silence now, unless explained, would be fairly liable to the contruction that my views had undergone some change in the lapse of years. Your letter affords an opportunity of explanation without seeming obtrusiveness on my part.

I gladly therefore avail myself of it in this reply. I was out of the State attending the Baptist Convention at Washington when the campaign was inaugurated. Ever since my return, May 20th, I have been confined to my bed by an attack of acute muscular rheumatism.

Moreover my loyalty to organization inclined me to allow the executive committee, chosen in convention, to mature their own plans and direct their execution. Somebody must be vested with authority and leadership to which the rank and file should submit; thereby all pulling together to secure the desired result.

These facts explain my silence, hitherto. I have been, however, neither inattentive nor uninterested. You may rest assured that my attitude toward

the Liquor Traffic has been in no way modified.
Time and observation confirm the conviction which
warmed my heart in 1887.

No one objection urged against prohibition then
has gained strength by lapse of time, while many
which were then urged with so much confidence and
zeal are now generally recognized as lighter than
chaff. They are no man's slogan now.

On the other hand the reasons for prohibition
urged in that campaign are to-day immovable as
granite and sanctified by experience. How well do
I recall them. To-day with more than pristine force
they commend themselves to the judgment of men
and the approval of God. Among the salient points
may be cited a few:

1. The Liquor Traffic as a business, outside of
the reasonable exceptions provided for in the Local
Option law, is essentially evil and lawless.

2. When it is licensed for revenue, it establishes
that most entangling and dangerous of all alliances,
a union of whisky and state. By license the state
becomes the partner of the saloon and throws its
aegis of endorsement and protection over a business
which debauches its citizens, corrupts public morals,
ruins the home and undermines its security and stability. Unquestionably the license makes the business
reputable so far as the State can confer respectability. The signification of any license granted by the
State and from which it derives revenue, is forcibly
expressed by Mr. Jefferson in his remarks on lotteries:

"This, then, is a declaration by the nation, that
an act was not immoral of which they were in the
habitual use themselves, as a part of the regular means
of supporting the government. The tax on the vendor of the ticket was their share of the profits, and
if their share was innocent, his could not be criminal."
(See Jefferson's works, Vol. 9, p. 502.)

Though I speak merely as a citizen, yet one who
believes in God, I cannot refrain from repeating an
inquiry propounded in a book, which many, at least,

hold sacred: "Shall the throne of iniquity have fellowship with thee, which frameth mischief by a law?"

3. The liquor traffic corrupts the purity of the ballot box. In all cities and with the ignorant and depraved everywhere is this self-evident.

4. Its plea for existence on the ground of revenue is deceitful, misleading and desperately wicked, since it dries up legitimate sources of revenue and destroys the forces and capacities which create revenue, while at the same time imposing an onerous burden of taxation on the community to maintain courts, jails and police, made necessary by its own ill effects on society.

5. By natural affinity it attracts to itself and associates with it all other forms of evil. Prostitution, gambling, misrule, anarchy and murder make the saloon their headquarters.

6. The system of license, and particularly of high license, centralizes the business, resting it mainly in a few great monopolies and money corporations. These more and more control the whole business, making the average saloon keeper only an agent. This makes combination and organization easy. This doubles the danger of the business as a political factor, gives it power to control or defeat legislation and to nullify judicial decisions. It is the license that thus makes it an awful and perpetual menace against the state and society. As a sad and fearful illustration of the potency and deadliness of its hostility behold its effect on the politicians! How few of them dare to open their mouths except as its advocate. A common street argument with the youthful and ambitious aspirant for office is the degrading threat but thinly disguised as a prophecy: "If you vote against whisky you need never run for an office."

But I forbear to enlarge. In a word it is the enemy of the home, the foe to labor, the corrupter of youth, the shame of gray hairs, the dread of mothers and wives. My deep and solemn conviction is that the safety of society, the purity of the ballot-box and the stability of government require the suppression of the traffic by law. Hence, very heartily do I extend to your committee such co-operation on my part as ability will allow and as may coincide with your plan of the campaign.

Very truly yours for Prohibition,

B. H. Carroll

XVII

LOCAL OPTION AND THE COURT OF CRIMINAL APPEALS

(The Standard's Query Department, April 12, 1906.)

From several sources inquiries come to this department concerning the decisions of this court on local option cases. The number, quality and variety of these inquiries indicate not only a deep and widespread interest in the matter, particularly in religious circles, but also indicate that the conviction is fastening upon some minds that this court, as now constituted, is hostile to prohibition legislation and the chief obstruction in the way of enforcing local option laws.

The further fact that this growing conviction in some quarters manifests the purpose to seek redress in popular elections by a change in the *personnel* of the court, embarrasses this writer no little in answering as best as he can the many questions received, since it is far from his purpose to enter into the political arena. Such purpose, therefore, is disavowed at the outset.

It is everywhere well known that while this writer is not a third party prohibitionist, he does favor both local option, and state prohibition by constitutional amendment, and rejoices at each prohibition victory, and has borne some humble part in a number of these struggles.

The many queries received may be condensed into the three following: First, what do you think of the decisions of the Court of Criminal Appeals on Local Option cases submitted to it? Second, do these decisions militate against either the legal capacity or the judicial integrity of its members? Third, what is the prohibition remedy for adverse judicial decisions?

The value of the reply to these questions will depend partly upon its being based on a fair induction of all the decisions rendered, and partly upon the writer's capacity to so analyze and classify these decisions as to make fair deductions from them. It was natural to expect that large vested interests, whose business is crippled by the enforcement of prohibition legislation would test before the courts every joint in the harness of the law. It was also natural to expect that decision on the various points raised would satisfy neither liquor men nor prohibitionists. These natural expectations have been fully realized in fact.

Under appeals from the lower courts, sometimes by prohibitionists, sometimes by liquor men, many decisions have been rendered by this court in the last twelve years on a great variety of distinct points. The decisions have not all been one way. In quite a number of cases the contentions of the prohibitionists have been sustained; in a less number of cases the contentions of the liquor men. A glance at the more important groups of cases so decided will be helpful toward a fair answer to the questions propounded.

The writer, himself, feeling somewhat sore on some of the decisions adverse to prohibition contentions, was constrained in fairness to the court to seek a summary of all the decisions. Quite a number of these decisions are now before him, and are thus classified as

DECISIONS OF THE COURT.

1. Is the law constitutional?
2. Has it been superseded by subsequent election laws?
3. On definition of terms, i. e., what constitutes intoxicating liquors?
4. The extent of prohibtion, i. e., does it destroy rights of property in liquor in local option

districts and forbid the privilege of cold storage with or without compensation?

5. On the application of the law, i. e., concerning the constitutionality of bunching precincts in ordering elections. This decision came on secondary legislation and really touches constitutionality.

6. On the validity of the various elections held under the law.

7. On the place of sale in C. O. D. shipments: (a) Without a previous order; (b) with a previous order. The questions involved in this group of decisions may be otherwise stated, viz., in a C. O. D. shipment is the common carrier the agent of the purchaser or of the seller? Again it may be thus stated: When is a sale through a C. O. D. shipment consummated? i. e., when delivered to the purchaser or when delivered to the common carrier?

8. What is a sale? i. e., does an exchange of property for whisky constitute a sale of whisky?

Perhaps all of the more important decisions may be grouped under these classifications. Looking now at the decisions thus numbered, in groups, which and how many have sustained the contentions of the prohibitionists, and which and how many have sustained the contentions of the liquor men? All of the decisions coming under groups, 1, 2, 3 and 8 have altogether sustained the contentions of the prohibitionists. In nearly all the cases coming under group 6 and in some of the cases coming under group 7, the decisions also favored the prohibition contentions.

To sum up: In perhaps not more than a half dozen cases out of many, have the decisions been adverse to prohibition contentions, and of these half dozen only one continues to create deep dissatisfaction; time and the decisions of the other courts having vindicated the holdings of this court on nearly all of the unsatisfactory decisions. The one great exception will be considered later.

On the other hand, the decisions have sustained

the contentions of the liquor men altogether on the cases coming under groups 4 and 5 and in one case under group 6, and in all cases under group 7, classification "b." In other words,

First, the Court of Criminal Appeals has decided that the local option law is constitutional against the contention of the liquor men that the exemption of the sale of intoxicants for medical and sacramental purposes nullified its constitutionality.

Second, the court has decided for the prohibitionists on the question of the supercession of the law, the liquor men contending that the subsequent Terrell Election law superceded the prohibition law of holding elections.

Third, the court has decided in favor of the prohibition contention on definition of terms, that is to say, the liquor men vainly sought refuge before the court under the vagueness of what constitutes intoxicating liquors.

Fourth, in nearly all of the cases where elections have been held and their validity has been assailed by the appeals of the liquor men, the court, in its decisions, has favored the contention of the prohibitionists.

Fifth, in the case of C. O. D. shipments without a previous order from the purchaser, the court has favored the contention of the prohibitionists that place of sale was at point of delivery and therefore a violation of the law in local option districts.

Sixth, the court has favored the contention of the prohibitionists where attempt has been made to shelter under exchange of property as not constituting a real sale.

On the other hand, in deciding the extent of prohibition, the court has favored the contention of the liquor men that the law did not destroy their right of property in liquor in local option districts nor forbid the privilege of cold storage with or without compensation. Again the court has favored the contentions of the liquor men in their construction of the act of the legislature with reference to bunching precincts in holding elections, and it has favored the contention of the liquor men in deciding that in C. O. D. shipments packages shipped upon a previous order, the place of sale was at the point of delivery to the common carrier and not to the purchaser.

In referring to the decisions of the court in the groups of cases cited, the majority decision is meant, there being three judges in the court; sometimes one of them would dissent from the other two.

Now in the light of this analysis of the decisions a reply is made to the questions. It is important to bear in mind that it is not the province of the Court of Appeals to make laws but to interpret them as made, and also that it is the custom of all courts to rely much on precedents.

That is to say, they look to the past decisions of their own court and similar courts in other states, and to the Supreme Court of the United States, in determining what contentions have been adjudicated and what legal principles have been established. Perhaps all courts carry this deference to precedents sometimes to the verge of subserviency, but the custom is there, and the reason of it is obvious, and in the main, commendable.

It must be also borne in mind that legislative enactments are seldom prepared by men as competent to frame a law as distinguished jurists are to interpret it when made, and that the wording of the law in its making is never so thoroughly tested as in the interpretation before the courts. The history of legislation is replete with instances of hasty and imperfect laws.

With so much premised, it is evident that the first two questions may be answered together. The decisions, considered altogether, do not indicate either an incapable or a partisan court. Of course both the prohibitionists and the liquor men have been dissatisfied with some of the decisions. So far as the writer, who is not a lawyer, can judge, all the decisions of the court unsatisfactory to prohibitionists have been accepted ultimately except those on C. O. D. packages with a previous order; in other words, while this writer was dissatisfied with several other decisions, he has about reached the conclusion that the decisions were either right or else with such a weight of probability in their favor they may be counted as settled, and he is frank to admit the ability of the court to buttress even its decision in the C. O. D. package cases with an overwhelming array of precedents.

To the writer's mind, however, the law principle is wrong, no matter how much buttressed by precedents, that makes the place of sale in C. O. D. shipments, with a previous order, at the point of delivery to the common carrier. The writer looks at this not at all as a lawyer but as the case appeals to the common sense of the people. To him it seems that if a man orders goods without the State, and especially where this order is based upon the solicitations of an agent in the State, unless the contract specifies that the sale is consummated when the package is put in the hands of the carrier, then the law ought to be, if it is not, that the obligation to pay the order does not mature until the purchaser has received in good order what he had ordered.

Common men do not feel that they owe for things never delivered; they do not feel that the carrier is their agent nor that they are responsible for damage or loss in transit. It is also supposed that the merchant himself, if a good business man, would know that his shipping trade through a common carrier, would suffer if his rule be to make the purchaser responsible before he received the goods. Again it is believed that a large shipper, familiar with the details of transportation, can better

hold the carrier responsible than the individual purchaser, profoundly ignorant of such details, and also
of the methods of recovery in case of loss. Yet a-
gain, the individual purchaser, making only an oc-
casional order C. O. D., is, as a rule, barred from
recovery of loss in transit because it will cost him
more than his one small matter is worth, and put
him to an amount of trouble and loss of time invoking the machinery of the law in seeking redress.
The shipper is not so barred, because of the volume
of his business.

It is upon this point that the writer's own mind
is most dissatisfied with the decisions of the court.
This dissatisfaction is intensified when the effect of
the decision in a very large measure nullifies the
prohibition law, and in a measure subverts the very
principle upon which local option rests, the right
of the people to determine by legislation what is for
their best interests. Particularly the writer believes
that in such a case as came up from Hill county,
briefed by his friend, Judge Greenwood, the contention of the prohibitionists should have been sustained, it being both easy and consistent to lean
toward the side of the people in a case stripped to
a bare principle.

But to answer the second question more particularly, the writer does not believe that this is
a partisan court. Whatever may be the opinion of
the members of this court on the advisability of
prohibition legislation, it is believed that when the
interpretation of that legislation comes before them,
their decision will be, not on the line of what they
wish the legislation to be, but upon the line of what
it is, fairly construed.

This leads to the answer of the third question:
"What is the prohibition remedy under adverse judicial decisions?" The writer is sure that the cause
of prohibition will not gain strength with thoughtful
minds by ill advised and intemperate criticism on
the integrity of the judges. That course is always

hazardous since it loosens the foundation's of government by destroying the sanctity of law in the minds
of the people. A better remedy must lie in perfect-
ing inadequate legislation.

The wisdom of the prohibitionists should center
on the point of devising a law that will both stand
the tests of the higher courts and also protect prohibition from nullification of the popular will by
invasions of liquor syndicate's whose *habitat* is outside of Texas. The limitations of state power, the
laws of inter-state commerce, the complications arising from the co-existence of both state and federal
courts create great but not necessarily insuperable
difficulties in the way of adequate legislation.

Prohibitionists must cultivate patience. Their
adversary is great. Dissatisfaction with one judicial
decision should not stop us from giving the court
fair credit for all favorable decisions. We should be
careful to note the significant and encouraging fact,
that during the twelve years this court has been deciding pro and con on different points, our cause
has made phenomenal progress. The law has been
fairly well enforced in many counties. Both the
feasibility and wisdom of the legislation i's day by
day receiving wider recognition.

Wisdom should suggest that the growing hold of
our cause on popular favor should not be weakened
by any extreme course likely to create distrust of
our principle's in sober minds. It is not denied that
a judge may be incapable, and may be so blinded by
partisan judgment that his decisions obstruct enforcement of law. Nor is it denied in such case
that a change in the *personnel* of the court should be
made in the appointed way. But it is claimed that
in such case the evidence should be clear and con-
vincing.

The method of securing judges by popular election is, to say the least, of questionable wisdom. A
jurist should be as far as possible from the demagogue. The very idea of a candidate for a judicial

position making a popular canvass is repugnant to the nature and sanctity of the office. A candidate who even impliedly precommits himself to a line of decisions in advance of each special case that may come before him, advertises his disqualification for the office.

XVIII

THE PROHIBITION OF THE LIQUOR TRAFFIC

(An address at the auditorium in Waco, Sunday afternoon, April 14, 1907.)

I have actively participated in four prohibition contests. In the first two, we lost; in the second two we won. But the greatest victory of all was in the defeat in 1887. The state of my health forbids an active participation in this campaign. What I now 'say is for the purpose of alignment: that everybody may know where I stand.

As briefly as possible I wish to answer six questions, state some underlying principle's of prohibition and make a short argument on one proposition.

QUESTIONS.

First, Is it right to use the Lord's day for discussion of political measures? Ordinarily the Southern preacher's answer to this question would be an emphatic "No." But we must distinguish before making that answer absolute and exceptionless. Technically and etymologically any public measure submitted to the decision of the ballot is political, but some public measures may be of such nature in themselves, and may be presented for consideration under such conditions, as to divest them of that ordinary political character obnoxious to Sunday discussion. Such, in my judgment, is the prohibition measure now pending in McLennan County.

This measure is not merely a moral one, and not only touching a business which has no natural right to existence, but it is,

First, dissociated from partisan politics, i. e., the object of the discussion is not to "boost" or set back any recognized political party, seeking governmental control, whether the Democratic party, the Republican party, or even the Prohibition Third party.

Second, it is dissociated from any candidacy for office whatever. As individuals some Democrats like myself will support the measure; others will oppose it. Likewise some Republicans will support and some oppose. And while what is called the Third Party Prohibitionists (numbering at the last presidential election about forty in this county, I believe) may not as individuals divide their vote on this measure, they know that individual Democrats and Republicans aligned with them on this non-partisan issue will not only resume alignment with their own parties on really political issues; but they also know that just to the extent that non-partisan prohibition measures prevail, precisely to that extent is the necessity for their existence as a political party removed and their hope of political supremacy as a party destroyed.

To illustrate my conviction on this point by the expression of a mere opinion, I think a great majority of the Republicans in this county, counting both black and white, will vote the anti-prohibition ticket. But that does not make anti-prohibition a Republican party issue, any more than the very few Third Party Prohibitionists' support of this measure make it their party issue.

But not even this argument will justify a service to-day that loses sight of the Christian spirit of the day. It is the New Testament Sabbath and the instruction given, together with the spirit in which it is given and received, must harmonize with the day. Never since I became God's minister, have I used the ministerial office or the Lord's day to promote partisan politics.

This distinguishing between the etymological sense of a word and its partisan application fully answers the absurd criticism in the papers of President Brooks' statement, "It is democratic for the majority to rule." He might have quoted Thomas Jefferson verbatim. He did not mean to affirm, nor was he properly understood to mean, that while majority rule is a democratic principle that meant that every expression of majority put the partisan Democratic party in power.

Second, Is it right for a church to discipline a man for voting on this measure pro or con? My an-answer is "No." A church may lawfully discipline a man for drunkenness, for frequenting saloons, for keeping saloons, or for renting property to saloons. But no human wisdom can forecast the possible evils likely to arise from disciplining men for their vote on measures of public policy. It might happen that some Republican church in the North might so conceive the voting of the Democratic ticket to be an act of such unrighteousness as to make it a test of fellowship. Or it might so happen that some church in the South, overwhelmingly Demo-cratic in its constituency, might conceive the voting of the Republican ticket an act of such unrighteous-ness as to make it a test of fellowship. There are possibly in every community at least a very few Christian men, themselves sober men, never enter-ing a saloon for any purpose and never renting property to one and abhorring the traffic, who yet may honestly question the expediency of this measure, without being influenced in that ques-tioning by a selfish commercial spirit. I have, I think, known a few such men. I know many hundreds who count themselves in this number without any just title to the classification.

Third, Should this be a campaign of personalities? Emphatically, "No." This answer is based primari-ly and mainly on principle. But even expediency demands it so far as prohibitionists are concerned. They cannot afford to enter such a contest. Those of them who are Christians are debarred by conscience from pushing such a contest to its logical results. And hence prohibitionists invite disaster when they use this weapon.

Fourth, What, then, should be the spirit of this campaign? First of all, every prohibitionist should fully concede to his opponents what he claims for himself, the inalienable right of every citizen to formulate his own judgment and to vote according to its dictates. To those of you who are Christians I would urge that you avoid every thought or word or deed that will leave you at the end of the campaign with a lower grade of spirituality. Upon all of you I would urge a white heat spirit of enthusiasm without acrimony. You not only cannot hope to win without enthusiasm but what is much more important, you cannot without it conduct a campaign of education that will profit in future campaigns.

Moreover, your enthusiasm must not demand as a condition of its exercise that you gain a majority of votes in this election. You may or may not win. But you will win a great victory if you succeed in lifting the canvass up to a higher plane of right spirit and sound argument, and thereby make real progress toward future success. Unquestionably our great defeat in 1887 was the greatest victory on this line. That campaign has been bearing fruit ever since. It was the real foundation of every subsequent victory at the ballot box.

Fifth, What is the issue? This is a vital question. Ah, me! if you prohibitionists would but manifest the great wisdom of sticking to the text! From many directions and by many adroit expedients of your opponents you will be tempted into by-paths of discussion on irrelevant matters, well calculated to sidetrack you from the real issue and vainly dissipate your forces. These adroit expedients are distributed from a national arsenal of munitions and weapons always full, always ready for use, forged by minds of extraordinary and trained intelligence, and employed when distributed by experts in practical politics.

It is regarded as the highest strategy of diplomacy to cause a divergence from the main question that will cause the people to lose sight of it. I recall, when in 1887 my old friend, John H. Reagan, Postmaster General of the Confederacy, United States Senator, and by all odds the leading Democrat of his time, a man whose record was never spotted, said to me in his own home town on the occasion of public addresses by both of us, that a United States Congressman was loading up especially for my discomfiture and that as soon as he arrived a debate would be arranged on a challenge from him. I asked him to explain the "loading up." "Why," he says, "the liquor dealers' attorney in Washington City, Mr. Schade, not only keeps on hand all kinds of printed matter, specially prepared for prohibition campaigns but takes pleasure in furnishing these forged thunderbolts to the anti-prohibition speakers and papers."

Already in this campaign have we come in contact with the munitions and weapons distributed from a central arsenal. And unquestionably the most effective of these consists of catch-words and brief documents to divert the mind of the voter from the main issue. Hence the importance of the answer to the question, What is the issue?

This issue concerns a business only. It is confined also to a sale only. This measure neither prescribes nor proscribes what any man, woman or child shall eat, drink, wear or buy. It touches sale only. If this measure should prevail any man in McLennan County might stand at mid-day on the streets of Waco, and in the presence of every county and municipal officer take a drink of alcoholic stimulants without violating this particular law.

The highest judicial decisions declare that this particular business has no natural right to existence. Moreover, some of the strongest anti-prohibitionists, for example, the Houston Chronicle in the last week's issue publicly declared that there is no moral defense for the business. Other anti-prohibitionists declare that unless it mends its ways there can be no defense of any kind. So strong an anti-prohibitionist as United States Senator Charles Culberson, at the recent State Democratic Convention, rebuked it for its interference with politics and openly threatened it with destruction by an indignant people if it did not keep out of politics.

I would say to those who base its only defense on the hope of its reformation that by its very nature it is irreformable. Like an india rubber ball, it may indeed yield for the moment to external pressure, but the moment the pressure is removed, it resumes its original state. It is inherently lawless. It is incapable of either repentance or reformation.

To those who base its defense on its keeping out of politics I would say that by its nature and by its artificial tenure of life it cannot keep out of politics. It must be, if it lives, a power in politics, and ever increasing in municipal, legislative and judicial politics or it must die.

Require a fish to live out of water; demand of an eagle that he shall not swoop with beak and talon on his natural prey; order a rattle snake, when stepped upon, not to sound his alarm by shaking its tail, or exposing his obtruding fangs, but do not be so illogical and foolish as to say, "O Saloons, amend your ways and keep out of politics!" It is both illogical and unfair to demand amendment on the part of the liquor business or to require it to keep out of politics. It is foolish to expect that it will ever do either. The question recurs, Shall we vote to continue licensing the saloon business which has no natural rights, and is irreformable, inherently lawless, and cannot keep out of politics?

Nor is this all the question. By its nature, this business expressed in saloons habitually associates itself with other evils, obnoxious to law and to the public welfare. For example, gambling. The saloon is not merely the habitat and Gibraltar of gambling, but it genders gambling and by its secretive methods evades the law against it and protects it even by violence. A notable instance occurred recently in Fort Worth. There can be no permanent enforcement of the law against gambling in cities while the saloons survive there.

Already the law puts an exclusive brand on this business. The banks, the mercantile houses, indeed every other form of business is exempted from this peculiar brand. On every election day, knowing it to be a menace to pure decisions at the ballot box, the law seals the doors of all the saloons: "No sale to-day." Moreover, while the officers of the law find no difficulty in enforcing the statute against sales by other business enterprises on Sunday, it has ever been impossible to keep the lid down for any length of time on the saloon business that day. How important it is, then, that every voter should shut his eyes and his ears to every side-tracking issue and allow this one issue alone to fill his vision and his hearing.

The solemnity of this solitary issue is not yet fully stated because the saloon is more dangerous in all the directions of its evil influences now than it formerly was. The space of time allotted to this address forbids an elaboration of the proof on this point. I call your attention to a magazine article, some years ago by Alton Locke, over the pseudonym of Petroleum V. Nasby. The article confines itself to a solitary point, viz., the great modern change in the centralization and ownership of the liquor business. In earlier years each man who desired, did his own manufacturing and each saloon keeper was the owner of his own stock. Therefore, it was far more difficult to organize the saloon forces for evil work. There were so many owners; they were so far apart; it took so much longer time and was so much more difficult to bring a vast number of individuals into effective organization for aggressive work. But under present conditions the entire business is controlled by a few syndicates, representing practically the power of a complete monopoly.

In aggressive movements now there is one great money power. There is only one or two controlling minds to govern. Preparations for war are always complete so that within twenty-four hours the entire power of the liquor business in the United States can be brought to bear on a single election in any county or upon any legislature, or upon controlling the appointment of the judiciary. So that there is continual and complete readiness at the touch of a button to bring the power of this great combination to bear at any one point on the whole length of the national firing line.

When you make this fight, you are not merely fighting the hurtful commercial spirit of Waco, forced into line by the saloon power, nor are you merely fighting a few licensed saloons in this city, nor the little campaign fund that can be gathered in this county, but you are fighting the entire power of the great national monopoly. It is this wonderful transformation in the saloon business by which retailers generally are mere agents in business of a single power, that it becomes such a menace in politics.

So that to fairly state this issue, our question would be, Shall we vote to continue the license of the liquor traffic in McLennan County, seeing that it is a business without natural right, that it is inherently evil and irreformable by nature, that it cannot keep out of politics, that necessarily it is associated with all other vices and immorality, that it breeds crime and vice in every direction and protects them from enforcement of law, that it is now in this county the expression of the aggressive force of a great national syndicate, representing incalculable wealth and incalculable power and always ready at all points along the whole line of battle from ocean to ocean. That, fellow citizens, is our issue.

My sixth and last question is, Is it in harmony with the Democratic principle of local option to vest in the county-site alone the decision as to the continuance of the legalized liquor traffic within its bounds? Is the hue and cry raised by the anti-prohibitionists that local option means for each precinct to determine for itself alone this question in its own bounds alone? This is the most notable case of special pleading ever known to campaign subterfuges. The constitution adopted mainly by the Democratic party, the clause in that constitution touching local option written by a Democratic hand, and the special statutes that carry out the constitutional principle, every one of them without exception, puts a county vote on the continuance of this business as an essential part of local option principle and law.

This is not merely true as to the constitutional and statutory declarations, but it is true in principle. The very existence of the county-site depends upon its indissoluble relations with the people of the whole county. Its local property is enhanced by county benefactions in the erection of county buildings and county courts. It is to the county as the heart is to the arterial system.

The fact that it has a special municipal government in no way destroys these vital relations with the county, nor neutralizes the reciprocal obligations arising from these relations.

The county-site cannot make the evils of this traffic terminate in itself. It cannot exempt the country people from footing the bills of costs arising from the evils of this business in the city. It cannot safeguard the people of the county from the dangers of the city traffic in this business.

The Times-Herald has declared, and rightly so, that the county is a unit. It is true without that declaration. And he who argues against the force of this unity on the subject of the liquor traffic in the county-site closes his eyes to logical truth and uses a campaign subterfuge for blinding the eyes of the people.

PRINCIPLES.

Having answered these six questions, I now wish to barely set forth some of the principles underlying the prohibition of the liquor traffic. In the statement of these principles I confine myself to citations from the civil law of an ancient nation which has been the groundwork of the civil law of all subsequent nations, really great in history.

The first principle is expressed in the following statute: "And if an ox gore a man or a woman to death, the ox shall be surely stoned, and its flesh shall not be eaten; but the owner of the ox shall be quit. But if the ox was wont to gore in time past and it hath been testified to its owner, and he hath not kept it in, and it hath killed a man or a woman; the ox shall be stoned and its owner shall be put to death."

The application of this principle to the present case is, that this liquor ox has not only gored its millions to death, but knowing that this ox was wont to push with its horns, it has been testified by thousands and in ten thousand ways to the owners and in spite of this testimony the goring unto death continues.

The second principle is expressed in this statute: "If fire break out and catch in thorns so that the stacks of corn or the standing corn, or the field, be consumed therewith, he that kindled the fire shall surely make restitution."

The application of this principle to the matter in hand is tremendous in its force. This liquor traffic fire is not an accidental fire, nor the result of mere carelessness, as in the case of the statute cited, but it is a deliberate incendiary fire. It has been kindled with the full knowledge that its wide-spread sparks, diffused by the gales of passion and appetite and greed, shall not merely burn the thorns that enclose the field. We might well let it burn if it were limited in its consumption to the thorns. But it is fore-known and fore-calculated that the sparks of this fire shall hail the stars in their height and reach the whole county in their extent, and shall kindle a conflagration that will paint hell on the sky and will blast the earth over which its consuming waves have passed. Not only stalks of corn feed this flame and stalks of corn in the country, not only standing corn, not only the field itself, in the country, but the homes of the people, and not merely the houses in which they live, but the men, women and children that live in the houses.

The third principle is expressed in a statute thus expressed substantially: If a man be found slain, and it be not known who hath slain him then the elders and the judges of the cities surrounding the place of the murder shall determine by measurement which city is nearest to the site of the murder, and then, after a sacrifice, they shall wash their hands and shall take oath over the dead man before God, that they are innocent of his blood. In later times and in other nations, when a murder had been committed, and the slayer was unknown, all suspected persons were required to come and lay their hands upon the body of the victim, trusting that God himself would cause the wounds to open and flow blood when the real murderer touched his victim.

Let us apply this principle of the law of this ancient nation to the notable case in Fort Worth. I was myself standing not far away when an honorable and faithful officer of the law, Jeff McLean, was shot to death on the street in open daylight, because, in obedience to the law, he had suppressed the adjunct gambling saloon. This murder was followed by the shooting down of a friend of the officer. In this case the hand which directly brought about this murder was well known and so far the law cannot apply, since he himself died in process of arrest.

But there remains yet another question to be considered: Did no guilt attach to the city in which it occured as *particeps criminis?* If the mayor and all the officers of the municipality had been compelled to go and lay their hands upon the dead body of Jeff McLean and then lift them up to heaven and make oath before God that they were in all respects guiltless of the blood of this man, could they in view of the legalized traffic in their midst have made this oath to God? Unquestionably there is municipal responsibility for every crime which takes place in a city.

The fourth principle is expressed in this curse: "Cursed be the man that riseth up and buildeth this city by laying its foundations in the blood of his first-born and setting up its gates in the blood of his youngest son."

The application of this principle is that in building up cities men shall not disregard the righteous principles upon which alone the prosperity of the cities shall depend; that no exigency for building up a city justifies the securing of its prosperity by the ruin of the family. The sweep of the principle extends from the first-born to the youngest son, that is, all the children. There can be no question that the history of the liquor traffic furnishes thousands of instances where men shut their eyes to everything but commercial prosperity, the buildding up of the city by any means that will bring money and add to wealth, have while securing that prosperity in these ways, laid the foundation in the blood of the first-born and set up the gates in the blood of the youngest son.

The fifth principle is expressed in statutes forbidding the setting of traps and deadfalls along the thoroughfares where all the people must walk to their daily business and in the statute which forbids the digging and leaving uncovered any pit into which a thoughtless animal or human may fall.

The application of this principle to the question in hand, presents a case more horrible than running the Indian gauntlet. The unarmed captive was compelled to pass down a street of men, ranged on either side, all ready to smite him, as he, staggering under blows from right or left, attempted to reach the goal of safety. Even the children cannot go from their homes to the public schools without passing through the gauntlet of saloons on either side.

The sixth principle, which is the last that this space permits to be stated, is expressed in the solemn question from the lips of a man of this ancient nation: "Shall the throne of iniquity have fellowship with thee that frameth mischief by a law?"

This principle supposes two diverse kingdoms of good and evil. There is a throne of righteousness over the good kingdom and a throne of iniquity over the evil kingdom. The question then is, Shall the throne of iniquity that maketh mischief by a law have fellowship with the throne of righteousness? This question takes cognizance of a civil matter, the enactment of a law that generates mischief.

In the application of this principle, the legalizing of the liquor traffic for the purposes of revenue, knowing that it genders crime, is the framing of mischief by a law. The penalty involved is that the city which frames this mischief by a law loses fellowship with the throne of righteousness and the loss of that fellowship entails the result expressed in these words, "Except the Lord keep the city the watchman waketh but in vain."

That is to say, that, though the police system be as Argus with a hundred eyes, and be as Briareus with a hundred hands, neither its vigilance nor its power can save the city from violence which is out of fellowship with the throne of righteousness. It is not only true that righteousness exalteth a nation, but it is true that righteousness exalteth a city. While there is in any sense of government of God, there must be both municipal, state and national responsibility on matters of civic righteousness.

So far in this discussion I have answered six questions and stated six principles. Now, I wish to make a brief argument on a solitary

PROPOSITION.

It is far more important to the citizens in the country that prohibition should prevail in the city than in all the country precincts of a county. This argument must needs be so concise as to be but terse expressions of thought without elaboration.

First, Prohibition in country precincts does not diminish the amount of the sale of liquor. It simply crowds into one place in the county all of the dealers of the traffic. Therefore the great whisky syndicate is but little concerned about the prevalence of prohibition in country precincts. There is no diminution of the volume of their business and there is a saving of expense to them in offices and in salesmen. That is why victory is so easy in a country precinct election.

Second, It has been an injustice on the part of the country precincts to dump into the county-site the whole volume of this business, making it impossible to have good city government.

Third, the attempt to break up this traffic by mere country precinct elections is like trying to kill a tree by threshing off a few of its leaves and breaking a few of its twigs. If the tree be evil, the axe laying at its root should be used to cut it down in its body.

Fourth, the countryman's vital interest in this matter has been somewhat expressed in the answer to one of the questions, that the county-site cannot make the evils of the traffic terminate in the city. They necessarily extend to the country. Nor can it exempt the man in the country from footing the bill of costs which result from prosecuting the violations of law brought about through this traffic.

Fifth, the cities are the centers, and in many respects, the basis and heart of national life. This at least is true to such an extent that it is impossible to reform a nation whose cities are corrupt. All efforts to reform New York State, for example, must fail as long as New York City remains corrupt.

Sixth, we cannot reform the city while the legalized saloon remains. I do not say that the liquor traffic constitutes the whole of city corruption. But it is in some way or other indissolubly connected with the most of city corruption and certainly to such an extent as to make city reformation impossible while the saloon remains.

The very foundations of national life are being undermined by a corrupt ballot. The ballot in the country may be approximately pure, but will be without power to effect the needed purity while the spirit and intent of the law of the ballot is violated in cities. And it is impossible to have a pure ballot in any city where the legalized saloon remains.

Already you have had brought to your attention as an illustration of this thought that the liquor traffic in violation of law has obtained control of the purchasable vote of the county by paying the poll-tax of a number great enough to constitute a balance of power in any election. The history of this transaction, as set forth in the public prints, is not only the most horrible illustration of the demoralization of the ballot law that I have ever known, but it makes it almost impossible to hope that our national life can be perpetuated since its prosperity depends upon the purity of the ballot.

And you must not forget that, while the primary object of this purchase of, say in round numbers, fifteen hundred votes in McLennan County, was to anticipate the safe-guarding of the saloon in coming elections of this character, but that these fifteen hundred men are available in elections upon all other subjects and for all offices, and become the material through which the most untrustworthy politicians get into office.

Fellow citizens, we might as well face the issue now as hereafter; our whole nation is doomed unless we can attain to a higher civic righteousness. But when you consider the power of the great syndicated monopoly of the liquor traffic in affecting elections and legislation, the administration of the law, the judicial appointments to construe the law, and when you consider that the dominant commercial spirit of cities has only one standard and that a metallic one, does this business in our judgment increase our city prosperity in a financial way and particularly does it help us to pay our taxes? Now, when we consider these two things alone in which the people of the country are vitally interested, how can they divest themselves of responsibility at the ballot box for the continuance of this traffic in the county-site?

It is to be hoped that some competent mind in the interest of future contests on this line shall formulate the argument on the truth of the proposition set forth above that shall not be merely irrefutable but so popularized in its expression as to reach the heart and control the vote of every man in the county.

The country man is asked not to vote the liquor traffic out of the county-site because in the county-site the law cannot be enforced and that, too, after just assuring the country people that the reason they should have prohibition in the country precincts was that they had not there any police power to protect against its evils. But in this case they say to the country man, "It is impossible for all the powers of the county and of the municipal government to enforce the prohibition law in the city." The fact that these two appeals to the country man are contradictory is the least of their evil. When they make this argument, they not only virtually prophesy the ruin of the nation, but virtually threaten that ruin by a practically open announcement that this traffic will neither obey the law nor can be made to obey the law.

When they cite some town in which, as they claim, prohibition has been reconsidered at a subsequent election because of the impossiblity of its enforcement in that town, they seem not to see that they thereby advertise to all of the world, not only the shame of that town, but give all men due notice that it is not a desirable place for any good man's residence. It seems to me that any right thinking man, having a family to raise, should decline to live in a town that thus openly publishes its shame and advertises its disregard for law.

The last thought that I have time to express is on this line. Anti-prohibitionists claim that prohibition by a county does not diminish the sale and consumption of ardent spirits in that county. It is very difficult for the most charitable mind to conceive how any thoughtful man could believe such a statement, even when he utters it. But not to make a personal reflection, assuming that he does believe what he says, then you have a right to say that he is as credulous and gullible as a fledgling bluebird which opens its mouth for food, no matter who shakes the bush containing the nest. And I have a right to say, that while men may make this assertion, and for charity's sake you may concede that they believe it when they say it, that there is no necessity in the world for your stupidity to be so great as to believe the statement to be true.

You might by law, for example, forbid Mr. Sanger to have any country branch houses. This would but little diminish his trade in the county, if the law applied to all other merchants, since the people would come here to buy, if no neighborhood retail establishments could be set up. But you could not make Mr. Sanger believe that if his business was forbidden in both the country precincts and in the city, with due penalties of law attached to the sale, that he would sell as much as before. A peddler with a few of his goods might steal into the territory occasionally and clandestinely sell a few trinkets out of the pack that he carried on his back. Or skulking agents in the dark alleys of the town, at extraordinary hours, might surreptitiously get off a few articles, but he would never believe that this would give him the volume of trade without restrictions.

I close with the announcement that conscience and judgment and the love of civic righteousness constrain me to give my hand and my heart and my vote to the advocacy of this measure.

XIX

THE PENDING PROHIBITION ISSUE IN TEXAS

(An article in the Baptist Standard, April 13, 1911.)

This discussion considers only three questions:

I. Why is statewide prohibition better than local option?

II. Why is constitutional prohibition better than legislative prohibition?

III. Why Christian people, regardless of denominational lines, political affiliations or personal friendships, should vote for the pending amendment?

The first and second questions concern the citizen — the third the Christian citizen.

The form of the first question is unfortunate for the prohibitionists and of great advantage to the liquor interests, but it is unavoidable. It is unfortunate because as this battle will be fought it may be made to appear that those opposed to statewide prohibition are the champions of local option, whereas the majority of them hate it, and that those favoring statewide prohibition are opposed to local option, whereas virtually all of them favor it. The spectacle will be both curious and anomalous, the liquor interests extolling the excellencies of local option which they hate and the prohibitionists pointing out the defects of local option which they love.

The opportunity has come for the anti-prohibitionist, *per se,* and *all along the line,* to avoid the odium of direct advocacy of the liquor business and to range himself under the banner of local option. Not only so, but many thousands of voters not anti-prohibitionists *per se,* not champions of the liquor business, may be, can be and probably will be influenced to vote against Statewide prohibition under various pleas that will more or less satisfy their consciences. So that the advantage of position in this fight is with the liquor business.

It should be observed that in this preliminary statement of the position it is not charged that all who will likely vote against statewide prohibition are either financially interested in the liquor business, or are its advocates *per se*. Nor is it denied that there are some honest advocates of local option who may not yet be prepared to advocate the more sweeping measure of statewide prohibition. The contention is that the advantage of position is with the liquor business.

One other preliminary observation: The proposed amendment is aimed at a *business* hurtful to society and not at the men engaged in the business nor at the defenders of the business whatever the grounds for defense. The defense may be open, direct, intentional or it may be only consequential, logical or virtual without intent to help the business. With the internal motives or justifying pleas the amendment does not concern itself. It proposes merely to outlaw the business. Moreover, the amendment aims not at the personal habits of the citizen. It neither prescribes nor proscribes what a man shall eat, drink or wear or the limit of his expenses, as do the sumptuary laws of many schools dealing with minors.

Every man of intelligence knows that if the amendment should pass and become a part of the constitution, it would not be in violation of it for a man standing at midday in the streets, to pull out his bottle and take a drink with governor, legislator, sheriff, mayor and police looking on. The amendment does not say: "Thou shalt not *drink* whisky" but "Thou shalt not *sell* whisky in Texas." It is the business of selling aimed at. Indirectly and consequently temperance may well be promoted by the law and the weakest and most helpless may be well protected. But let every prohibitionist stress the issue: The proposed law seeks to abolish outright as a legal business, confessedly evil and lawless in spirit, the traffic in spirituous liquors which other laws hitherto have vainly attempted to regulate or restrict within safe bounds.

Having laid down these premises as to the advantage of position and the purpose of the law proposed, let us consider the three questions to which this particular discussion limits itself.

I. WHY IS STATEWIDE PROHIBITION BETTER THAN LOCAL OPTION?

1. Because, on the same underlying principles, it is an extension of the good of local option, a forward movement on the same lines. On underlying legal principles what is right in this direction for a precinct or county is certainly right for a state. And on the principles of the unit, or integer, the argument is stronger for the state than for the precinct, county or even nation. No one of the three is so much a unit as the state. The precinct and county are but fractions of a unit, the nation is a combination of associated units, on certain limited lines, as the name, "United States," clearly shows. Indeed, a state as a complete unit may do things in its own bounds that the nation can not do in the state bounds. The right of a state to abolish this business in its own bounds is more unquestionable than the right of the nation to abolish it in a particular state.

So that no argument is good for precinct or county prohibition that would not be stronger for the state and no objection against state prohibition can be reasonably urged that can not in its principles be shown to apply to precinct or county option. The verdict by majority in any of the three, precinct, county or state, may be shown to work a hardship on some people or some interests of the minority.

2. Both the rightfulness and propriety of state prohibition must be conceded as a guaranty to the right of county prohibition. The most spacious and plausible plea against State prohibition has been urged, as if irresistible and unanswerable in this form: "If Wise county wants prohibition, let Wise county have it. But let not Wise county and others desiring prohibition for themselves dictate it to Dallas, Tarrant and Bexar counties which do not desire it." Let it be repeated that this plea has been paraded as if self-evidently sufficient, indeed as axiomatic. Over and over again it has been asked triumphantly, "How can you answer that?" Here then is submitted a supreme answer.

The liquor business in the counties which don't want prohibition will not allow the counties to have it which do want it. What they claim for themselves as so sacred they deny to others. By all means, no matter how illicit, they continually seek to thwart and disrupt the verdict in the prohibition county. This unlawful aggression against the precinct-right is so pressed that to preserve the right the county must be carried, and so pressed against the county right that the state must be carried to preserve the county option. If the liquor interests in wet counties had respected the verdict of dry counties, there would be not only more sincerity but more force in their plea. If some Eastern county wants a hog law, the Western counties do not interfere. Why on this matter alone may not a county hold its option undisturbed? There is no such outside intrusion into and illicit disturbance of a county verdict, in other local matters.

The reason is obvious. Here is a business inherently and everywhere lawless. It has no god but greed and with a more than Eastern devotion kneels at the shrine of its idolatry. It has no motive but self-interest and hence respects no law either human or divine, except under compulsion. Therefore a dry county, in order to preserve its right to be dry must move out its fences. Just so the frontier counties of Virginia and Kentucky *had to send* George Rogers Clark to capture old Vincennes and other outlying districts in order to preserve their own homes and families from a barbaric foe that spared neither age nor sex.

Therefore Scipio, as a more effective *defense of Rome* at whose gates Hannibal was thundering *carried the war into Africa.* Either Rome must die or Carthage must be destroyed. Hence this specious and seemingly axiomatic plea, no matter how much whisky it may hold, will certainly not hold water.

3. Statewide Prohibition is better than county prohibition because of the nature of the power of the liquor business. This power largely resides in the fact that there is a union of whisky and State. If there be good reasons for opposing a union of church and State, much more for opposing a union of whisky and State. And if divorce of whisky and State be desirable the separation can be reached more readily and rendered more effective through the State, the real unit, than through its fractions, the precinct and county.

Paul said: "The strength of sin is the law." As well may one now say, "The strength of the liquor business is the law which unites this business with the State, which by division of proceeds in the name of revenue makes the state a partner in the buiness." The law in Paul's case was holy, just and good. The law in the latter case comes nearer to the prophetic and inspired question of the Psalmist: "Shall the throne of iniquity have fellowship with thee, which frameth mischief by a law?"

4. State prohibition is better than local option because the liquor business is now syndicated. It is a trust of such enormous capital and such con-

centration of power in a few hands, that it has become too formidable an adversary for any mere precinct or county to cope with for any length of time.

There was a time when almost every dealer in the business was an independent owner of the business he handled. Now all but a few are mere agents of a higher power, so that the business of a nation not only may concentrate its power against any precinct or county striking out for freedom, and may maintain hosts of expert legal counsel to try every issue before the courts, but also has factories for making ammunition and implements of war more formidable than the Krupp factory which furnishes big guns and munitions for the German army. Any speaker or paper against prohibition, may be supplied on short notice and to any amount, and of any kind, with guns and ammunition adapted to any kind of local condition from the headquarters' arsenals always full. Here always ready for use are shrewdly tabulated statistics, anecdotes and illustrations, quotations f r o m influential people, especially preachers, catchwords, outlines of argument, suggestions as to campaign methods, and withal those peculiar *"sinews of war"* so necessary in modern campaigns.

5. State prohibition is better than local option because it is the only hopeful way to carry the counties in which are cities. The latest census reports show that Fort Worth, Dallas, Houston, Galveston and San Antonio are practically the counties in which they are located. They have the overwhelming majority of voters in the county. And in every one of these cities the business is entrenched as the British in Gibraltar. Cities are like hearts — out of them are the issues of life or death for the State.

6. State Prohibition is better than Local Option because since the syndicating of the liquor business it has so entered politics as to become the balance of power in elections and legislation and

such a balance of power that counties and precincts can never reach the root of the matter. They may thrash off a few leaves and lop off a branch here and there, but the tree never stops growing. Personally, the business cares nothing about politics one way or another, except only as its own interests may be affected. It can with equal facility unite with Republicans or Democrats or Socialists to carry a point.

Here in Texas, with anything like a respectable division on other matters, any strong, popular Democratic candidate plus the liquor interest can beat the field. So in the legislature, given a respectable division on other matters, any strong, popular leader plus the liquor interest can carry or defeat a pending bill. Just here it may be said that it is useless to raise any cry against the business for entering politics. You may appropriately raise that cry against entering the business. But the business having been established it must enter politics, and stay in politics and hold the balance of power or die. With every man in the business an independent owner of his business they could not combine so as to enter politics effectively, but syndicated into a trust, the purse held by a few and the directing minds being few, the business has so entered politics as to seriously menace the perpetuity of free institutions.

It has already come to pass that free institutions are shut up to one of two alternatives: The liquor business must be put out of politics or free institutions must die. But what precinct or county election on this matter can drive this business out of politics? Therefore, State prohibition is better than local option.

While only a few of the most salient points have been considered, enough are here suggested to sustain the contention. So let us pass to the second question:

II. WHY IS PROHIBITION BY CONSTITUTIONAL AMENDMENT BETTER THAN LEGISLATIVE PROHIBITION, BOTH BEING GOOD AND STATEWIDE REMEDIES FOR AN ACKNOWLEDGED EVIL?

The answer is so obvious that a mere statement of facts is a sufficient argument.

1. Legislative prohibition does not take the disturbing matter out of politics but entrenches it there. The agitation never ceases. It enters into every election, State, municipal and county. With every ebb and flow of the political tide the legislature changes in personnel so that what it may do at one session, it may reverse at the next session. Hence legislative prohibition never did have the opportunity of a fair trial, in order to get a real test of its wisdom.

2. Constitutional prohibition affords a better opportunity. There is time to correct errors in the statutes which carry out the constitution. It is not claimed that even prohibition by State constitutions will have a perfectly fair trial so long as the United States government for purposes of revenue issues licenses for the territory of prohibition States. Of course this national license can not confer or enforce the right to sell in these States, but only exempts the holder from amenability to Federal law. Yet many people do not understand these distinctions, and so they become confused. The United States having sold the license and got the money, does not intervene to protect the culprit prosecuted under State law. The Nation does not care how many times the State in the exercise of her police power, convicts the holder of Uncle Sam's license.

Uncle Sam's license merely exempts from conviction under Federal law. Still Uncle Sam's license does bother and complicate matters in the minds of the people, and does operate to some extent in preventing State prohibition from having a fair trial.

If only Uncle Sam could be induced to withhold license in prohibition States and bar its transport over interstate lines it certainly would both simplify and help matters. But Uncle Sam wants the big revenue and so again illustrates the iniquity of the union of whisky and state.

III. WHY CHRISTIANS OF EVERY NAME AND FAITH SHOULD SUPPORT THE PENDING AMENDMENT?

It is wholly unnecessary for any Christian to enter a discussion as to whether the making, selling or using intoxicating liquors is a sin *per se* and under all circumstances. It is sufficient to know that this business as now conducted and under existing conditions is a menace to the home, the family peace and public morals; that it is associated with a group of evils that enhances its power and multiplies the hazards to public and private life, and happiness; that on the whole, and as conducted, it is a foe to grace and the gospel of the kingdom.

Under these conditions it is not required that you should classify yourself as either a fanatic or an extremist. But you are forced by the exigencies of the situation to vote for licensing this acknowledged evil with all its practical concomitants, thus riveting the bonds of the unity of whisky and State, or to vote to outlaw it as an evil business. You are not called on to outlaw people, but a traffic. You are not asked to denounce persons, but to vote against the continuance of a business under law sanctions. You are not asked to say by your vote that the pending measure is devoid of difficulties and objections.

No human wisdom can formulate a perfect law, or forecast all its consequences. In his history of England, Macaulay scores the brilliant Lord Halifax as an impractical statesman because his capacity for seeing objections prevented a hearty support of any measure proposed.

An incident will illustrate this point: A certain well known but somewhat eccentric doctor of divinity propsed marriage to an equally well known widow. She promptly replied: "Doctor, there are serious objections in my mind to marrying you." "What has that to do with the matter?" promptly countered the doctor. "Why, madam, I had a thousand objections to marrying you, but I *waived them* because of the greater reasons on the other side."

You are not asked to see in the passage of the amendment some particular advantage to a Methodist, or a Baptist, or a Presbyterian, or an Episcopalian, or a Roman Catholic, but as God's man to settle it in your heart on which side you should align yourself. There is not the slightest reason for you to go into subtle discussion of abstract theories. You have been to Dallas or Fort Worth or Houston or Galveston or San Antonio. In many of these places you have only to look around with the eyes of common sense to see the evil of this business, its corrupting associations, its demoralizing trend, its promotion of other vices, its unrestrainable lawlessness, its vicious control of popular elections, its menace to society, its hazard to the home, to the perpetuity of free institutions, the boys and girls it destroys, and then answer to your Christian heart: "Can I, as God's man, vote to further legalize this business?"

Your personal friendship for this or that congressman or senator has nothing to do with the matter. Your vote is neither intended to commend nor reflect upon any of them. None of them is a candidate for office in this election. Happily this election is dissociated from any candidacy for office and severed from all partisan politics. You are not called on to express sympathy for or alignment or grudge against Republican or Democrat or Socialist. This is one time you are free from all entangling alliances and may vote as God's man for or against a confessed evil. You know that if this time Christians vote together for this amendment it will be carried. You know that if it fails to carry many Christians will have voted against it.

To you above all men comes in a voice of thunder the question of the Psalmist: "Shall the throne of iniquity have fellowship with thee, that frameth mischief by a law?" Read Albert Barnes' great discussion of that text. Republish his sermon in your papers. Get the secular press in line with you, to republish Alton V. Locke's great magazine articles on the change of the situation as it affects the purity of the ballot and all politics by the syndicating of the liquor interest into a gigantic trust with millions of money and concentration of power, a trust so formidable, so vicious and corrupting in its interferences with politics, with municipal government, with legislation, with the executive and judicial power that the business must be outlawed or irretrievable disaster must overtake this republic — the last retreat of civil and religious liberty.

A great jurist of this State who heard me on these lines in '87, on the streets of one of Texas' leading cities, came to me after the speech and volunteered the statement: "You have surprised me. You have shaken my life-long convictions. You have evinced no fanatical spirit, indulged in no personalities, avoided extremes, and dispassionately discussed a very grave matter on fair and broad lines of thought and argument. What your lines of thought have suggested are more and weightier in the light of my experience and observation than even what you have said. I do not commit myself offhand to vote with you but I do not now see how I can vote against that amendment."

If, O Christian, this man should hesitate to align himself with the liquor interests, what shall be your attitude? Will any of the specious pleas so easily urged against the amendment, will any or all the objections to it occurring to your own mind or suggested by others, salve your conscience as God's man, if you ignore the evidently vicious trend of this business and the weight of probabilities in favor of employing some remedy more commensurate with the requirements of the case than local option can ever supply?